American Values

OPPOSING VIEWPOINTS®

Other Books of Related Interest

American Values

OPPOSING VIEWPOINTS®

Mary E. Williams, *Book Editor*

Bruce Glassman, *Vice President*
Bonnie Szumski, *Publisher*
Helen Cothran, *Managing Editor*

OPPOSING
VIEWPOINTS®
SERIES

GREENHAVEN PRESS
An imprint of Thomson Gale, a part of The Thomson Corporation

THOMSON

GALE

Detroit • New York • San Francisco • San Diego • New Haven, Conn.
Waterville, Maine • London • Munich

For more information, contact
Greenhaven Press
27500 Drake Rd.
Farmington Hills, MI 48331-3535
Or you can visit our Internet site at http://www.gale.com

Cover credit: © Comstock

LIBRARY OF CONGRESS CATALOGING-IN-PUBLICATION DATA

American values : opposing viewpoints / Mary E. Williams, book editor.
   p. cm. — (Opposing viewpoints series)
Includes bibliographical references and index.
ISBN 0-7377-2220-7 (lib. bdg. : alk. paper) —
ISBN 0-7377-2221-5 (pbk. : alk. paper)
   1. Social values—United States. 2. United States—Moral conditions. I. Williams, Mary E., 1960– . II. Series.
HN90.M6.A45 2005
303.3'72'0973—dc22   2004040520

Printed in the United States of America

"Congress shall make no law. . . abridging the freedom of speech, or of the press."

First Amendment to the U.S. Constitution

The basic foundation of our democracy is the First Amendment guarantee of freedom of expression. The Opposing Viewpoints Series is dedicated to the concept of this basic freedom and the idea that it is more important to practice it than to enshrine it.

Contents

Why Consider Opposing Viewpoints?

"The only way in which a human being can make some approach to knowing the whole of a subject is by hearing what can be said about it by persons of every variety of opinion and studying all modes in which it can be looked at by every character of mind. No wise man ever acquired his wisdom in any mode but this."

John Stuart Mill

In our media-intensive culture it is not difficult to find differing opinions. Thousands of newspapers and magazines and dozens of radio and television talk shows resound with differing points of view. The difficulty lies in deciding which opinion to agree with and which "experts" seem the most credible. The more inundated we become with differing opinions and claims, the more essential it is to hone critical reading and thinking skills to evaluate these ideas. Opposing Viewpoints books address this problem directly by presenting stimulating debates that can be used to enhance and teach these skills. The varied opinions contained in each book examine many different aspects of a single issue. While examining these conveniently edited opposing views, readers can develop critical thinking skills such as the ability to compare and contrast authors' credibility, facts, argumentation styles, use of persuasive techniques, and other stylistic tools. In short, the Opposing Viewpoints Series is an ideal way to attain the higher-level thinking and reading skills so essential in a culture of diverse and contradictory opinions.

In addition to providing a tool for critical thinking, Opposing Viewpoints books challenge readers to question their own strongly held opinions and assumptions. Most people form their opinions on the basis of upbringing, peer pressure, and personal, cultural, or professional bias. By reading carefully balanced opposing views, readers must directly confront new ideas as well as the opinions of those with whom they disagree. This is not to simplistically argue that everyone who reads opposing views will—or should—change his or her opinion. Instead, the series enhances readers' understanding of their own views by encouraging confrontation with opposing ideas. Careful examination of others' views can lead to the readers' understanding of the logical inconsistencies in their own opinions, perspective on why they hold an opinion, and the consideration of the possibility that their opinion requires further evaluation.

Evaluating Other Opinions

To ensure that this type of examination occurs, Opposing Viewpoints books present all types of opinions. Prominent spokespeople on different sides of each issue as well as well-known professionals from many disciplines challenge the reader. An additional goal of the series is to provide a forum for other, less known, or even unpopular viewpoints. The opinion of an ordinary person who has had to make the decision to cut off life support from a terminally ill relative, for example, may be just as valuable and provide just as much insight as a medical ethicist's professional opinion. The editors have two additional purposes in including these less known views. One, the editors encourage readers to respect others' opinions—even when not enhanced by professional credibility. It is only by reading or listening to and objectively evaluating others' ideas that one can determine whether they are worthy of consideration. Two, the inclusion of such viewpoints encourages the important critical thinking skill of objectively evaluating an author's credentials and bias. This evaluation will illuminate an author's reasons for taking a particular stance on an issue and will aid in readers' evaluation of the author's ideas.

It is our hope that these books will give readers a deeper understanding of the issues debated and an appreciation of the complexity of even seemingly simple issues when good and honest people disagree. This awareness is particularly important in a democratic society such as ours in which people enter into public debate to determine the common good. Those with whom one disagrees should not be regarded as enemies but rather as people whose views deserve careful examination and may shed light on one's own.

Thomas Jefferson once said that "difference of opinion leads to inquiry, and inquiry to truth." Jefferson, a broadly educated man, argued that "if a nation expects to be ignorant and free . . . it expects what never was and never will be." As individuals and as a nation, it is imperative that we consider the opinions of others and examine them with skill and discernment. The Opposing Viewpoints Series is intended to help readers achieve this goal.

David L. Bender and Bruno Leone,
Founders

Greenhaven Press anthologies primarily consist of previously published material taken from a variety of sources, including periodicals, books, scholarly journals, newspapers, government documents, and position papers from private and public organizations. These original sources are often edited for length and to ensure their accessibility for a young adult audience. The anthology editors also change the original titles of these works in order to clearly present the main thesis of each viewpoint and to explicitly indicate the opinion presented in the viewpoint. These alterations are made in consideration of both the reading and comprehension levels of a young adult audience. Every effort is made to ensure that Greenhaven Press accurately reflects the original intent of the authors included in this anthology.

Introduction

"Moral relativity leads to the degradation of the moral fiber of our society, penalizing anyone who dares to take a stand on moral grounds."

—Daniel Bagley

"Relativism must play a role in our analysis of moral and ethical issues. We don't live in a static world of absolutes."

—John Hamerlinck

A disturbing trend is prevalent in America's schools, claims *U.S. News & World Report* columnist John Leo. "Some students," he contends," are unwilling to oppose large moral horrors, including human sacrifice, ethnic cleansing, and slavery, because they think that no one has the right to criticize the moral views of another group or culture." Leo cites the example of a college student who personally deplored the Jewish Holocaust but could not admit that genocide was always wrong. "Of course I dislike the Nazis," the student explained to his professor, "but who is to say they are morally wrong?" According to Leo, the student held this opinion because he had actually been taught that no culture can be judged from the outside and that no individual should question the ethical standards of another.

Leo's claims about the pervasiveness of moral relativism—the belief that morality is a matter of individual choice—are backed by statistics. According to a 2002 Zogby International poll, 73 percent of American college seniors agree that the typical message they received about ethical issues in the classroom was "what is right and wrong depends on differences in individual values and cultural diversity." Leo believes that the prevalence of moral relativism is the result of two recent educational "fads": postmodernism, a theory rooted in the idea that there is no objective truth, and multiculturalism, an approach to teaching that highlights an awareness of minorities, women, and other historically oppressed groups. Critics maintain that postmodernism and multiculturalism place too much emphasis on tolerance, which can lead students to conclude that all opinions are equally valuable and that no one should judge the moral worth of any culture's beliefs or practices.

The biggest danger of moral relativism, critics assert, is that it refuses to support definite rules, making it difficult for people to condemn any behavior, no matter how evil. As philosophy professor Francis Beckwith states, "[If moral] life is only a matter of personal tastes, preferences, and orientations . . . , then we cannot tell young people it's wrong to lie, steal, cheat, abuse drugs, or kill their newborns." Leo, Beckwith, and others warn that moral relativism could undermine values that have long been highly regarded by Americans—particularly honesty, loyalty, religious faith, and a reverence for life.

Other social analysts, however, argue that the nature and purpose of moral relativism is deeply misunderstood by its critics. For example, writer John Hamerlinck contends that true relativists are not unethical, but simply believe that moral issues have few absolutes. He offers one scenario as evidence that morality depends upon circumstances: Suppose a murderer were stalking your friend—should you lie to the murderer about your friend's whereabouts? Hamerlinck asks: "How many people, Christian or otherwise, would not lie in that situation? Is lying therefore an absolute moral wrong? No, because ethics are inescapably situational. Although there is general agreement across the ideological spectrum that lying is wrong, there are still situations in which it is the morally correct thing to do."

Sociology professor William Tonso agrees with Hamerlinck and argues further that moral relativism should not be seen as a worldview or principle to live by, but an analytical process that one uses to make judgments. Social scientists studying the Nazi movement, for example, would need to analyze and understand the Nazi belief system prior to drawing conclusions about Nazism. They would need to keep their own personal views in check as they learn that Nazis considered exterminating Jews a moral act. As Tonso points out, "If . . . we're going to try to analyze, explain, and/or understand why people behave in ways that we find strange or wrong, we're going to have to relate to them by getting into their worlds. We can't afford to ethnocentrically assume that our ways are the only right ways. But to . . . *understand* [others] social-scientifically doesn't mean that we must personally *condone* what they do." Critics of moral relativism, he argues, have mistakenly concluded that the objectivity needed to analyze and understand others' opinions leads to acceptance of those opinions.

The contrasting views of morality and ethics posed by the above commentators come into play during debates about a wide spectrum of social issues. In the chapters What Values Should America Uphold? Is America in Moral Decline? How Should Patriotism Be Defined? How Can American Values Be Improved? the authors of *Opposing Viewpoints: American Values* provide a variety of perspectives on the state of political and moral values in the United States.

CHAPTER 1

What Values Should America Uphold?

Chapter Preface

One of the provisions of the First Amendment to the U.S. Constitution is that the government should "make no law respecting an establishment of religion, or prohibiting the free exercise thereof." This passage is often invoked in discussions about the religious liberty that Americans enjoy and in testimonials about the importance of the separation of church and state. As a result of the First Amendment, the U.S. government does not favor any one religion, nor may it use taxes to provide aid to any religion. The state may not participate in the activities of any religious organization, and people cannot be penalized for belief or nonbelief.

Because the population of the United States includes people of widely varying backgrounds, many Americans hold the separation of religion and state in high regard and believe that such a principle is essential to an open, pluralistic society. As American Humanist Association president Edd Doerr points out, "The American experience has proven that separation of church and state is best for religion, for democratic government, and for the liberties of the people." If the wall dividing religion and state were to break down, Doerr contends, the United States would be faced with two disturbing possibilities: the government might attempt to suppress certain religious beliefs and practices, and powerful sectarian interests could use the government to impose their beliefs on the population.

Some analysts, however, contend that the principle of church-state separation has been misinterpreted in a way that limits religious freedom. In the opinion of Alabama judge Roy S. Moore, American Christians and Jews are not allowed to express their beliefs at state-funded venues because church-state separation is usually taken to mean that government cannot support religion in any way. However, Moore asserts, the ideal of church-state separation was actually intended to keep the government from prescribing what one's faith should be—not to preclude people from publicly acknowledging God. According to Moore, America's founders did not believe that "all public worship of God must be halted; on the contrary, freedom to engage in such worship was the very reason for creating a doctrine of separation between church and state." But because the doctrine has been misconstrued, the government continues to ban religious activity in public venues, which in turn causes a general moral decline in America, concludes Moore.

The debate over the meaning of church-state separation highlights the question of what role religion should play in the public sphere. The following chapter offers disparate views on religion and other forces, such as capitalism and patriotism, that shape morality in America.

"*American patriotism has always been rooted in love of the principles upon which the nation was founded: liberty, equality, justice, and democracy.*"

Patriotism Should Be Promoted

William J. Bennett

Some Americans exhibit a startling ignorance of U.S. history and fail to appreciate their nation's values and ideals, writes William J. Bennett in the following viewpoint. Yet the United States deserves the pride of its citizens, he maintains, because it is the most democratic, tolerant, and prosperous nation on Earth. Americans need to learn and remember that their nation's founding principles of liberty and justice influence and benefit the entire world. If the need should arise, Bennett concludes, these American ideals are worth defending with one's life. Bennett is chair of Americans for Victory over Terrorism and codirector of Empower America, a policy organization in Washington, D.C. He is also the author of several books, including *Why We Fight: Moral Clarity and the War on Terrorism*.

As you read, consider the following questions:

1. According to Bennett, what percentage of surveyed college students know the name of the U.S. secretary of state?
2. What does the author's "gates test" reveal about the United States?
3. Why has Western civilization flourished in the past several centuries, in Bennett's opinion?

William J. Bennett, "A Nation Worth Defending," *USA Today Magazine*, vol. 131, November 2002, p. 10. Copyright © 2002 by the Society for the Advancement of Education. Reproduced by permission.

On Sept. 11, 2001, America suffered more civilian casualties than on any other day in its 226 years when terrorists hijacked jetliners and crashed them into the nation's financial and military centers. Only through the heroism and courage of passengers on one plane were they prevented from striking the nation's capital. For many—especially those who lived in the cities struck—the shock and horror of that day remain with them. For others, however, the memory has faded. I recently spoke with a radio station in Portland, Ore., and asked the host how Sept. 11 had affected them. Not much, he admitted: "We think it was more of an East Coast thing."

In one way, this is a great strength of America: We move on. It is also, though, a great weakness, especially at a time like this. As Americans, we must remember more than we do. The U.S. is, indeed, a nation worth defending, but one that, surprisingly, many Americans find themselves reluctant to defend.

American Ignorance

I am the chairman of Americans for Victory Over Terrorism (AVOT), dedicated to sustaining and strengthening American public opinion in the war on terrorism. We recently conducted a poll of college students to determine their knowledge of and attitudes about the war. What we found was disturbing:

• Less than half of those we surveyed could name the U.S. Secretary of State.

• About one-third could identify the prime minister of Israel and the U.S. Secretary of Defense.

• Approximately one-quarter could identify the three nations that Pres. Bush identified as the Axis of Evil.

• Fewer than 20% could name the American national security advisor and the United Nations' secretary-general. . . .

Moreover, of the 55 highest-ranked colleges and universities in the nation, not a single one requires students to take a course in American history in order to graduate. Only three require a course in Western civilization. This is cause for alarm, but it should not come as a surprise. The recently released National Assessment of Education Progress reveals that 57% of high school students are "below basic" in their knowledge of history. Just 18% of fourth-graders, 17% of eighth-graders, and 11% of 12th-graders score at the "proficient" level, the one at which the National Assessment Governing Board, the administrators of the tests, says all students should perform.

This historical ignorance is not merely of academic concern. It has real-world consequences. Returning to the AVOT poll, more than 70% of college students disagree—and 34% strongly disagree—that the values of the U.S. are superior to those of other countries. More than one-third disagree with the claim that, "Despite its flaws, the United States is the best country in the world." Eighty percent reject the claim that Western civilization, with its unparalleled achievements and human flourishing, is superior to Arab civilization. In what was perhaps the most-striking finding, one-third said that they would evade a military draft in the war on terrorism; another third would refuse to serve abroad; and just one-third would willingly go fight overseas.

Ideas, author Richard Weaver famously wrote, have consequences. Similarly, pernicious ideas have pernicious consequences. The idea that America is no better than any other nation is one pernicious idea; the claim that our values are no better than any other set of values is another; and the pernicious consequence of such ideas is that two-thirds of our college students—the future leaders of America—would refuse to serve in the military in a foreign country during the war on terrorism.

From what does this reluctance to defend America—morally and intellectually—arise? I would argue that it stems from a lack of education about America or, in some cases, a historically incorrect education about America, which is even worse. Education ought not be defined narrowly as the accumulation of knowledge; it also entails preparing a future generation of citizens. Education, by its nature, includes civic education. That is why, as the Greek philosopher Plato put it, the fundamental task of any regime is the education of the young. A nation cannot survive if its young are not intellectually and morally prepared to defend it.

What should children be taught about America? They

should be taught the truth about it. If we are a nation that was created by a political vision of equality and liberty, our story is the story of the struggle to realize that vision, those ideals. We have had our failures—some of them shameful—but never once have we lost sight of our moral ideals, which is why we have been able to transcend the stains on our record, foremost among them that of slavery. Who else among the world's nations could enter such a claim?

A Democracy to Be Proud Of

Our country is something to be proud of, something to celebrate. We should not shrink from saying so. A careful and close reading of our history demonstrates that we have provided more freedom to more people than any other nation in the history of mankind; that we have provided a greater degree of equality to more people than any other nation in the history of mankind; that we have created more prosperity and spread it more widely than any other nation in the history of mankind; that we have brought more peace and justice to the world than any other nation in the history of mankind; and that our open, tolerant, prosperous society is the marvel—and the envy—of the ages.

This is demonstrably true within our own borders. Outside those borders, we have been a beacon of freedom and opportunity to people throughout the world since the day of our creation. When people around the globe demonstrate in support of freedom and liberty, they do so with American icons and documents. I will never forget—we should never forget—how the brave Chinese students in Tiananmen Square faced off with tanks, armed with only a papier-mâché Statue of Liberty and a copy of the Declaration of Independence. Pernicious ideas have pernicious consequences, but good and noble ideas can have good and noble consequences, too.

The noble ideas of America have led to noble consequences and noble actions on our part. For example, in the 20th century alone, as one British columnist pointed out, Americans "saved Europe from barbarism in two world wars . . . [and] rebuilt the continent from ashes. They confronted and peacefully defeated Soviet Communism, the most murderous system ever devised by man. . . . America, primarily,

21

ejected Iraq from Kuwait and . . . stopped the slaughter in the Balkans while the Europeans dithered." This list could be extended tenfold and it would still be incomplete.

Put simply, America is the place people run to when, in hope or hopelessness, they are running from somewhere else. I have devised a simple test to illustrate this, the gates test, as I call it: If a nation were to have entirely free and un-fettered, unchecked and unpatrolled borders, would people come in or go out? If the U.S. opened its borders, there would be streams of people trying to enter the country. Even with border patrols and immigration policies, there are people trying to get in. Many of those people—both today and in decades past—have risked life and limb to flee re-pressive regimes like Cuba, China, and the Soviet Union to enjoy the freedoms and opportunities unique to America.

That these freedoms and opportunities are unique to America is not merely a conservative position. Listen to what former Senator (D.-N.Y.) and Ambassador to the United Nations Daniel Patrick Moynihan has to say on the matter: "Am I embarrassed to speak for a less than perfect democracy? Not one bit. Find me a better one. Do I suppose there are societies which are free of sin? No, I don't. Do I think ours is, on balance, incomparably the most hopeful set of human relations the world has? Yes, I do."

The Last Best Hope of Earth

It is starting from this bedrock understanding that an educa-tion in patriotism should proceed, for "what is taught will not be forgotten, and what is forgotten cannot be defended," as the American Council of Trustees and Alumni has put it. The job of educators—not just teachers, but parents and politi-cians as well—in our time is to make sure that these truths are not forgotten, that children learn that their great nation is, as Pres. Abraham Lincoln said, the last best hope of Earth.

There is much that can be taught to our children about Sept. 11. On that bloody day, we saw the face and felt the hand of evil, but we saw something else—heroism, courage, and honor.

We saw the firemen who rushed into the burning infernos of the World Trade Center as so many men and women were rushing out. We heard the audiotapes of the struggle on Flight 93, where men and women who expected nothing more than a normal cross-country flight came together to overpower the terrorists and keep that plane from being used as a missile. Today, we see the ongoing bravery of the men and women in our armed forces, risking their lives around the world to protect America and all that she stands for. Children will learn from that.

To learn from it, however, they must be reminded of it. If our children are not reminded of the heroism of Sept. 11, they will not learn to be brave. If they do not learn about the great and noble things our country has done, they will not learn to be patriotic. If they do not learn to be brave and patriotic, our nation is in grave danger. Today's children are tomorrow's soldiers, citizens, and leaders. They will be called on to defend our country—to defend their country—in the years to come. They must be prepared to do so.

The Value of Western Civilization

In order to do so effectively, we must all be able to see through fogs of moral obfuscation and political correctness. The reluctance of college students to state that Western civilization is superior to Arabic civilization is not surprising. A poll of students by the National Association of Scholars found that three-quarters of American college students say their professors teach them that right and wrong depend "on differences in individual values and cultural diversity."

You may recall that, shortly after Sept. 11, Prime Minister Silvio Berlusconi of Italy asserted that Western civilization was "superior" to that of Islam. As you might expect, the guardians of political correctness were up in arms: "Simply unacceptable" and "deeply dangerous rantings," complained the *Washington Post;* other newspapers and international leaders added that the comments were "absurd," "Neanderthal," "disgusting," and "outrageous." Put aside the question of whether or not Berlusconi's remarks were impolite. Let us focus on the simple question of whether they were true. Could it be that Western civilization is superior to Islamic civilization?

It is hard to look at the world today and argue otherwise.

The Western world has led to a standard of living unprecedented in human history. It has guaranteed a system of rights and liberties for men and women that are all but unknown in the Islamic world. Scientific progress has benefited rich and poor, young and old. Throughout the Western world, there is a degree of human flourishing that is absent from the suffering that characterizes life for so many in the Middle East.

Mill. © 2002 by Eleanor Mill. Reproduced by permission.

As Berlusconi said, Western civilization "has guaranteed well-being, respect for human rights and . . . respect for religious and political rights"; it is a "system that has as its values understandings of diversity and tolerance." While he was wrong to deny that such "respect for human rights and religion" existed anywhere in the Islamic world, it is all but inarguable that such respect is the rare exception, and certainly not the rule.

Islamic civilization does have a noble heritage of its own. During the Middle Ages, for instance, Islamic scientists and philosophers made contributions that remain valuable even to this day. Yet, for the past several centuries, as historian Bernard Lewis reminds us, Islamic civilization has remained stagnant, while the West has flourished.

I believe that one reason the West has flourished while Islamic civilization has remained stagnant is that the spirit of democracy and liberty in the West encourages questioning, debate, and progress. To learn about the value of capitalism, we read John Stuart Mill and Karl Marx. To learn about the value of the religious life, we read Thomas Aquinas and Voltaire. To learn about the ends of politics, we read Aristotle and Machiavelli. To learn about the value of warfare, we read Homer and Erasmus. To learn about the worth of sexual fidelity, we read Leo Tolstoy and James Joyce. Our intellectual tradition is not monolithic; it is, rather, an ongoing conversation.

Diversity and Tolerance

As Berlusconi said, we value diversity—especially intellectual diversity—and tolerance in a way that no other civilization does. Western civilization demands inquiry and leads to progress at a rate and of a degree previously unknown to mankind. The tradition of liberalism and liberal education in the West has led to human liberation to think, dream, and live.

As political philosopher A.E. Murphy put it many decades ago, "We do not understand the ideals of other cultures better by misunderstanding our own or adequately enrich an intercultural synthesis by offering to it anything less than the best we have. That best is the theory and practices of intellectual, moral, and political freedom, in a form and at a level which neither medieval, Mexican, Manchu, nor Muscovite culture has so far equaled."

I will never forget the scenes that occurred in November,

2001, when the American and British forces liberated Kabul, [Afghanistan]. Burqas were cast off; beards were shaved; and television sets were dug out of the ground. An entire city celebrated the end of strict Islamic rule. This event suggested that cultures and values are not so different after all. Anyone who saw the pictures of people suddenly free to speak, dress, learn, work, and worship as they saw fit would be hard-pressed to deny a universal human longing for freedom.

Simple honesty ought to compel us to state—and to do so proudly—that, while the longing is universal, one particular cultural tradition has most fully nourished it. That tradition is ours, and students ought to be made aware of it and its successes.

The Importance of Patriotism

Since the beginning of time, political philosophers have recognized the importance of patriotism. One of Plato's first dialogues is the Crito, which is subtitled "The Duty of a Citizen." This is an account of a conversation between Socrates and his friend Crito, as the former awaits his execution by the city of Athens. Crito and other friends have devised a plan by which Socrates can escape the unjust sentence handed down. Yet, Socrates demurs. He explains to Crito that the city—even if it has done him harm—has a claim to his loyalty that surpasses even death. The state, Socrates reminds Crito, "brought [me] into the world, and nurtured and educated [me]." Escaping would be nothing more than "running away and turning your back upon the compacts and agreements which you made as a citizen." It would, in short, be a repudiation of his entire life. In his later and more-detailed studies of government—*The Republic* and *The Laws*—Plato spends a great deal of time discussing the moral and civic education of the young, training them to be good citizens. His pupil Aristotle, too, was concerned with these matters, as a cursory reading of *Politics*—and even the Nicomachean *Ethics*—will show.

In modern times, however, that notion of patriotism has been eviscerated. British philosopher Thomas Hobbes, in *Leviathan*, declared that government is simply a construct designed to ameliorate the state of nature—which in life, in his memorable phrase, is "solitary, poor, nasty, brutish, and short." By identifying the fear of death—especially violent, painful death—as man's most-powerful passion, Hobbes argued that the state had claim to our allegiance only as long as it preserved our life. Once it no longer could protect us, we no longer were obliged to obey its commands; the paramount right of nature of man is to "preserve his own life and limbs, with all the power he hath." There is no good greater than one's own life; no man can surrender his right to self-preservation. On this theory, then, we would understand it if our troops were to surrender and join forces with the enemy when outnumbered in combat. It would be, Hobbes writes, cowardly—but not unjust.

That is not the understanding of patriotism accepted by our Founding Fathers, though. They created a nation to which they were dedicated, even at the cost of their own lives. It was a concept of a country—and a claim to loyalty—larger than one's own security and prosperity. Indeed, the Founders themselves risked their lives for this nation and its principles long before it ever existed. Many of the signers of the Declaration of Independence lost their homes, property, and fortunes. They were aware of the risk they were taking. As one signer put it, he and his fellow revolutionaries knew they were signing their own "death warrants." Nathan Hale famously remarked that his only regret was that he had but one life to give for his country—one that had yet to exist.

American Principles

Still, in an age where so much has been scorned for so long, what does patriotism mean? Do we stand with American naval officer Stephen Decatur when he exclaimed, "Our country, may she always be in the right, but our country, right or wrong!"? Does patriotism mean that we love America simply because it is our country? In a word, no. The American understanding of patriotism has never been as simple as that.

American patriotism has always been rooted in love of the principles upon which the nation was founded: liberty, equality, justice, and democracy. We are, in that sense, unique—our patriotism is not parochial. That is to say, our love for America does not necessarily entail dislike of other countries.

Indeed, insofar as those nations share our principles—think, for instance, of Great Britain or Israel—we consider them our friends and allies, not competitors.

Upon the death of Sen. Henry Clay, Abraham Lincoln said that Clay "loved his country partly because it was his own country, but mostly because it was a free country . . . he saw in [the advancement of his country] the advancement, prosperity, and glory of human liberty, human right, and human nature." American prosperity is not good only for America, it is good for the rest of the world, for the principles of America are good for the rest of the world. That is a lesson that we adults—as much as our children—need to learn, remember, and, when called upon, defend.

"*We must say goodbye to patriotism because the world cannot survive indefinitely the patriotism of Americans.*"

Patriotism Should Be Abandoned

Robert Jensen

Robert Jensen is a journalism professor at the University of Texas at Austin and the author of *Writing Dissent: Taking Radical Ideas from the Margins to the Mainstream*. In the following viewpoint Jensen examines the concept of patriotism in light of America's response to the terrorist attacks of September 11, 2001. While a majority of citizens defined patriotism as support for U.S. government policy and the use of military force in response to terrorism, those with antiwar views argued that it was patriotic to question government policy and oppose the use of force. Jensen maintains that uncritical loyalty to one's government is wrong; however, he also questions the alternative concept of patriotism because it seems to presume that freedom and justice are uniquely American ideals. Ultimately, patriotism is a chauvinistic concept that should be discarded. If Americans want to be truly just, Jensen concludes, they must transfer their love of country to a love of the world.

As you read, consider the following questions:

1. How did Emma Goldman define patriotism, according to the author?
2. What analogy does Jensen use to illustrate what he sees as a flaw in the peace and justice movement's definition of patriotism?

Robert Jensen, "Saying Goodbye to Patriotism," *The Witness*, vol. 85, March 2002, pp. 17–20. Copyright © 2002 by the Episcopal Church Publishing Company. Reproduced by permission.

In a review that I wrote [in the summer of 2001] of a book about the history of wartime restrictions on U.S. news media, I faulted the author for accepting American myths about the nobility of our wars and their motivations. I challenged his uncritical use of the term patriotism, which I called "perhaps the single most morally and intellectually bankrupt concept in human history."

By coincidence, the galley proofs for the piece came back to me for review a few days after [the September 11, 2001, terrorist attacks]. I paused as I reread my words, thinking about the possible reactions given the reflexive outpouring of patriotism in the wake of the terrorist attacks. I thought about the controversy that some of my antiwar writing had already sparked on campus and beyond. I thought about how easy it would be to take out that sentence.

But I let it stand, for a simple reason: The statement was true on September 10, and after September 11 I'm more convinced it is true.

I also believe that nestled in the truth of that assertion is a crucial question for the U.S.-based peace movement, one that we cannot avoid after 9/11: Are we truly internationalist? Can we get beyond patriotism? Or, in the end, are we just Americans?

That is a way of asking whether we are truly for peace and justice. I mean the statement to be harsh because the question is crucial. If in the end we are just Americans, if we cannot move beyond patriotism, then we cannot claim to be internationalists. And, if we are not truly internationalist in our outlook—all the way to the bone—then I do not think we can call ourselves people committed to peace and justice.

Let me try to make the case for this by starting with definitions.

My dictionary defines patriotism as "love and loyal or zealous support of one's own country." I will return to that, but it also is important to look at how the word is being used at this moment in this country, where there are two competing definitions of patriotism circulating these days.

It's easy to get a handle on this use of the word. Just listen to the president of the U.S. speak, or watch TV. This view of patriotism is simple: We were attacked. We must defend ourselves. The only real way to defend ourselves is by military force. If you want to be patriotic, you should—you must—support the war.

I have been told often that it is fine for me to disagree with that policy but that now is not the time to disagree publicly. A patriotic person, I am told, should remain quiet and support the troops until the war is over, at which point we can all have a discussion about the finer points of policy. If I politely disagree with that, then the invectives flow: commie, terrorist-lover, disloyal, unpatriotic. Love it or leave it.

This kind of patriotism is incompatible with democracy or basic human decency. To see just how intellectually and morally bankrupt it is, ask what we would have said to Soviet citizens who might have made such an argument about patriotic duty as the tanks rolled into Prague [Czechoslovakia] in 1968. To draw that analogy is not to say the two cases are exactly alike but rather to point out that a decision to abandon our responsibility to evaluate government policy and surrender our power to think critically is a profound failure, intellectually and morally.

Patriotism as Critique of the War Effort

Many in the peace-and-justice movement, myself included, have suggested that to be truly patriotic one cannot simply accept policies because they are handed down by leaders or endorsed by a majority of people, even if it is an overwhelming majority. Being a citizen in a real democracy means exercising judgment, evaluating policies, engaging in discussion, and organizing to try to help see that the best policies are enacted. When the jingoists start throwing around "anti-American" and "traitor," we point out that true patriotism means staying true to the core commitments of democracy and the obligations that democracy puts on people. There is nothing un-American, we contend, about arguing for peace.

This may be the best way—perhaps the only way—to respond in public at this moment if one wants to be effective in building an antiwar movement; we have to start the discussion where people are, not where we wish people were. But increasingly, I am uncomfortable arguing for patriotism,

31

even this second definition. And as I listen to allies in the peace-and-justice movement, I wonder whether that claim to patriotism-as-critical-engagement is indeed merely strategic. Critical questions come to mind: Are we looking for a way to hold onto patriotism because we really believe in it? Is there any way to define the term that doesn't carry with it arrogant and self-indulgent assumptions? Is there any way to salvage patriotism?

I have come to believe that invoking patriotism puts us on dangerous ground and that we must be careful about our strategic use of it.

At its ugliest, patriotism means a ranking of the value of the lives of people based on boundaries. To quote Emma Goldman: "Patriotism assumes that our globe is divided into little spots, each one surrounded by an iron gate. Those who had the fortune of being born on some particular spot, consider themselves better, nobler, grander, more intelligent than the living beings inhabiting any other spot. It is, therefore, the duty of everyone living on that chosen spot to fight, kill, and die in the attempt to impose his superiority upon all others."

People have said this directly to me: "The lives of U.S. citizens are more important. If innocent Afghans have to die, have to starve—even in large numbers—so that we can achieve our goals, well, that's the way it is." We may understand why people feel it, but that doesn't make such a statement any less barbaric.

But what of the effort to hold onto a kinder and gentler style of patriotism by distinguishing it from this crude nationalism? What are the unstated assumptions of this other kind of patriotism? If patriotism is about loyalty of some sort, to what are we declaring our loyalty?

If we are pledging loyalty to a nation-state, what if that nation-state pursues an immoral objective? Should we remain loyal to it? If our loyalty is to a specific government or set of government officials, what if they pursue immoral objectives or pursue moral objectives in an immoral fashion?

Loyalty to American Ideals?

Some suggest we should be loyal to the ideals of America, a set of commitments and practices connected with the concepts of freedom and democracy. That's all well and good; freedom and democracy are good things, and I try to not only endorse those values but live them. I assume we all try to do that.

But what makes those values uniquely American? Is there something about the U.S. or the people who live here that makes us more committed to, or able to act out, the ideals of freedom and democracy—more so than, say, Canadians or Indians or Brazilians? Are not people all over the world—including those who live in countries that do not guarantee freedom to the degree the U.S. does—capable of understanding and acting on those ideals? Are not different systems possible for making real those ideals in a complex world?

Freedom and democracy are not unique to us; they are human ideals, endorsed to varying degrees in different places and realized to different degrees by different people acting in different places. If Americans do not have a monopoly on them, why express a commitment to those ideals by talking of patriotism?

A Helpful Analogy

An analogy to gender is helpful. After September 11, a number of commentators have argued that criticisms of masculinity should be rethought. Though masculinity is often defined by competition, domination and violence, they said, cannot we now see—realizing that male firefighters raced into burning buildings and risked their lives to save others—that masculinity can encompass a kind of strength that is rooted in caring and sacrifice?

Of course men often exhibit such strength, just as do women. So, the obvious question arises: What makes these distinctly masculine characteristics? Are they not simply human characteristics?

We identify masculine tendencies toward competition, domination and violence because we see patterns of different behavior; men are more prone to such behavior in our culture. We can go on to observe and analyze the ways in which men are socialized to behave in those ways, toward the goal of changing those destructive behaviors.

That analysis is different than saying that admirable human qualities present in both men and women are somehow primarily the domain of one gender. To assign them to a gender is misguided, and demeaning to the gender that is then assumed not to possess them to the same degree. Once we start saying "strength and courage are masculine traits," it leads to the conclusion that woman are not as strong or courageous. To say "strength and courage are masculine traits," then, is to be sexist.

Kirk. © 2002 by *The Toledo Blade*. Reproduced by permission.

The same holds true for patriotism. If we abandon the crude version of patriotism but try to hold onto an allegedly more sophisticated version, we bump up against this obvious question: Why are human characteristics being labeled American if there is nothing distinctly American about them?

If Americans argue that such terminology is justified because those values are realized to their fullest degree in the U.S., then there's some explaining to do to the people of Guatemala and Iran, Nicaragua and South Vietnam, East Timor and Laos, Iraq and Panama. We would have to explain to the victims of U.S. aggression—direct and indirect—how it is that our political culture, the highest expression of the ideals of freedom and democracy, has managed routinely to go around the world overthrowing democratically elected governments, supporting brutal dictators, funding and training proxy terrorist armies, and unleashing brutal attacks on civilians when we go to war. If we want to make the claim that we are the fulfillment of history and the ultimate expression of the principles of freedom and justice, our first stop might be Hiroshima [Japan].

Patriotism Is Chauvinism

Any use of the concept of patriotism is bound to be chauvinistic at some level. At its worst, patriotism can lead easily to support for barbarism. At its best, it is self-indulgent and arrogant in its assumptions about the uniqueness of U.S. culture.

This is not a blanket denunciation of the U.S., our political institutions, or our culture. People often tell me, "You start with the assumption that everything about the U.S. is bad." But I do not assume that; it would be as absurd a position as the assumption that everything about the U.S. is good. No reasonable person would make either statement.

That does raise the question, of course, of who is a reasonable person. We might ask that question about, for example, George Bush, the father. In 1988, after the U.S. Navy warship *Vincennes* shot down an Iranian commercial airliner in a commercial corridor, killing 290 civilians, Bush said, "I will never apologize for the U.S. of America. I don't care what the facts are."

I want to put forward the radical proposition that we should care what the facts are. If we are to be moral people, everything about the U.S., like everything about any country, needs to be examined and assessed.

There is much about this country a citizen can be proud of, and I am proud of those things. The civil liberties guaranteed (to most people) in this culture, for example, are quite amazing.

There also is much to be appalled by. The obscene gaps in wealth between rich and poor, for example, are quite amazing as well, especially in a wealthy society that claims to be committed to justice.

This need not lead to moral relativism. We can analyze

35

various societies and judge some better than others by principles we can articulate and defend—so long as they are truly principles, applied honestly and uniformly. But we should maintain a bit of humility in the endeavor. Perhaps instead of saying "The U.S. is the greatest nation on earth"—a comment common among politicians, pundits and the public—we would be better off saying, "I live in the U.S. and have deep emotional ties to the people, land and ideals of this place. Because of these feelings, I want to highlight the positive while working to change what is wrong."

We can make that statement without arrogantly suggesting that other people are inherently less capable of articulating or enacting high ideals. We can make that statement and be ready and willing to engage in debate and discussion about the merits of different values and systems.

We can make that statement and be true internationalists, people truly committed to peace and justice. If someone wants to call that statement an expression of patriotism, I will not argue. But the question nags: Why do we need to call it patriotism? Why do people hold onto patriotism with such tenacity?

Love or Leave "It"?

When I write or talk with the general public and raise questions like these, people often respond, "If you hate America so much, why don't you leave?"

But what is this America that I allegedly hate? The land itself? The people who live here? The ideals in the country's founding documents? I do not hate any of those things.

When people say to me "love it or leave it," what is the "it" to which they refer? No one can ever quite answer that. Still, I have an answer for them.

I will not leave "it" for a simple reason: I have nowhere else to go. I was born here. I was given enormous privileges here. My place in the world is here, where I feel an obligation to use that privilege to be part of—a very small part of, as we all are only a small part—a struggle to make real a better world. Whatever small part I can play in that struggle, whatever I can achieve, I will have to achieve here, in the heart of the beast.

I love it, which is to say that I love life—I love the world in which I live and the people who live in it with me. I will not leave that "it."

I also can say clearly what the "it" is not.

The America I love is not this administration, or any other collection of politicians, or the corporations they serve.

It is not the policies of this administration, or any other collection of politicians, or the corporations they serve.

The America I love is not wrapped up in a mythology about "how good we are" that ignores the brutal realities of our own history of conquest and barbarism.

I want no part of the America that arrogantly claims that the lives and hopes and dreams of people who happen to live within the boundaries of the U.S, have more value than those in other places. I will not indulge America in the belief that our grief is different. Since September 11, the U.S. has demanded that the world take our grief more seriously, and when some around the world have not done so we are outraged.

But what makes the grief of a parent who lost a child in the World Trade Center any deeper than the grief of a parent who lost a child in Basra when U.S. warplanes rained death on the civilian areas of Iraq in the Gulf War? Or the parents of a child in Nicaragua when the U.S. terrorist proxy army ravaged that country? Soon after 9/11, I heard a television reporter describe lower Manhattan as "Beirut on the Hudson." We might ask, how did Beirut come to look like Beirut, and what is our responsibility in that? And what of the grief of those who saw their loved ones die during the shelling of that city?

Where was the empathy of America for the grief of those people?

Certainly we grieve differently, more intensely, when people close to us die. But the grief we feel when our friends and neighbors became victims of political violence is no different than what people around the world feel when their friends and neighbors die. Each of those lives lost abroad has exactly the same value as the life of any one of us.

Goodbye to Patriotism

September 11 was a dark day. I still remember what it felt like to watch those towers come down, the darkness that settled over me that day, the hopelessness, how tangible death felt—for me, not only the deaths of those in the towers but also the deaths of those who would face the bombs in the war that might follow, the war that did follow, the war that goes on.

But I also believe there is a light shining out of that darkness that can lead Americans to our own salvation. That light is contained in a simple truth that is obvious, but which Americans have never really taken to heart: We are part of the world. We can no longer hide from that world. We cannot allow our politicians, generals and corporate executives to do their dirty business around the world while we hide from the truths about just how dirty that business really is. We can no longer hide from the coups they plan, the wars they start, the sweatshops they run—from the people they kill.

For me, all this means saying goodbye to patriotism.

That is the paradox: September 11 has sparked a wave of patriotism, which has in many cases been overtly hateful, racist and xenophobic. A patriotism that can lead people to say, as one person wrote to me, "We should bomb [Afghanistan] until there's no more earth to bomb."

But the real lesson of September 11 is that if we are to survive as a free people—as decent people who want honestly to claim the ideals we say we live by—we must say goodbye to patriotism. Patriotism will not relieve our grief, but only deepen it. It will not solve our problems but only extend them. There is no hope for ourselves or for the world if we continue to embrace patriotism, no matter what the definition.

We must give up "love and loyal or zealous support of one's own country" and transfer that love, loyalty and zealousness to the world, and especially the people of the world who have suffered most so that we Americans can live in affluence.

We must be able to say, as the great labor leader of the early 20th century Eugene Debs said, "I have no country to fight for; my country is the earth, and I am a citizen of the world." I am with Debs. I believe it is time to declare: I am not patriotic. I am through with trying to redefine the term to make sense. There is no sense to it.

That kind of statement will anger many, but at some point

we must begin to take that risk, for this is not merely an academic argument over semantics. This is both a struggle to save ourselves and a struggle to save the lives of vulnerable people around the world.

We must say goodbye to patriotism because the kind of America the peace-and-justice movement wants to build cannot be built on, or through, patriotism.

We must say goodbye to patriotism because the world cannot survive indefinitely the patriotism of Americans.

"Capitalism raises and transforms selfishness and acquisitiveness into higher purposes."

Capitalism Is Beneficial

John Mueller

In the viewpoint that follows, John Mueller maintains that free-market capitalism is beneficial because it creates wealth and fosters economic growth. Moreover, contrary to what critics claim, capitalism usually inspires honest and virtuous business behavior. Entrepreneurs who do succumb to greed and deceit act foolishly, Mueller points out, because honesty and industriousness in business ventures are more wealth-enhancing in the long run. Since humanity is flawed, capitalism cannot ensure absolute economic security, Mueller grants. However, institutions like capitalism and democracy do not require human perfection in order to be generally beneficial. Mueller is a political science professor at Ohio State University and the author of *Capitalism, Democracy, and Ralph's Pretty Good Grocery.*

As you read, consider the following questions:
1. In Mueller's opinion, what can result from negative images of capitalism?
2. What is the lesson offered by Ralph's Pretty Good Grocery store's slogan, according to the author?
3. According to Mueller, what is one way to discern that a social institution is sound?

John Mueller, "Democracy vs. Capitalism," *The American Enterprise*, vol. 13, March 2002, p. 44. Copyright © 2002 by The American Enterprise Institute for Public Policy Research. Reproduced by permission of *The American Enterprise*, a magazine of Politics, Business, and Culture. On the Web at www.TAEmag.com.

D emocracy and free-market capitalism seem to suffer from image problems—opposite ones, as it happens. Capitalism is much better than its image; Democracy has turned out to be much worse.

Although capitalism is generally given credit, even by its detractors, for generating wealth and stimulating economic growth, it is commonly maligned for its seeming celebration of greed. But actually, capitalism tends to reward business behavior that is honest, fair, civil, and compassionate. And it inspires a form of risk-taking behavior that can often be characterized as heroic.

Meanwhile, democracy is often presented in an idealized manner: citizens participating on an equal basis in enlightened deliberations about the affairs of governance. By contrast, actual democracy is often found to be disappointingly wanting—notable chiefly for discord, inequality, apathy, hasty compromise, political and policy ignorance, and manipulative scrambling by "special interests."

These disconnections can have significant, and often detrimental, consequences. The mismatch of capitalism with its image can damage economic growth, particularly if people in business embrace the negative stereotype. The democracy mismatch can eventually result in cynicism about the democratic process—even to the point of inspiring a yearning to scrap the system entirely.

Capitalism Rewards Virtue

The negative perception of capitalism has been propagated not only by communists and socialists, but by the church, popular culture (including capitalist Hollywood), intellectuals, aristocrats, and often by capitalists themselves—particularly those who have lost out in the competitive process. Swindlers and moral monsters sometimes do become rich (in both capitalist and noncapitalist systems), but contrary to the popular notion, capitalism by its nature rewards many virtuous behaviors. It generally inspires industriousness, farsightedness, diligence, and prudence. Businesses have found that "Honesty is the best and most profitable policy," that "A happy employee is a productive employee," and that "The customer is always right." These are soundly practical guidelines, and part of a broader set of self-effacing moral principles that are, on average, wealth-enhancing.

This is not to say that capitalists necessarily and always behave virtuously. Many, indeed, have lied, cheated, acted shabbily, and let themselves be dominated by arrogance and ego. But such behavior is economically foolish.

Nor does the existence of the capitalist virtues mean that there is no room for government, or that capitalism can be entirely self-regulating. Societies may find it useful, usually for non-economic reasons, to use tax policy and regulation to redistribute wealth, to aid the unfortunate, to enhance business competition, to regulate for public health and safety, or to control undesirable side effects such as air pollution. Societies may also consider it desirable to ban or inconvenience the propagation of certain goods and services for which there is profitable demand—like drugs, pornography, prostitution, cigarettes, liquor, and gambling. And it should be emphasized that capitalists do not pursue virtue to the point of stupidity: Virtues do not require one to cut an unfavorable deal or trust a swindle.

But virtue is, on balance and all other things being equal, essentially smart business under capitalism: Nice guys, in fact, tend to finish first. Some scoundrels do become rich, even as some heavy smokers escape cancer. But just as smoking is [not], in general, good for your health, virtuous business behavior is, in general, good for your bottom line.

The Image Problems of Capitalism and Democracy

Capitalism's image mismatch can hamper economic development—because without the unacknowledged capitalist virtues, countries remain mired in poverty. Fortunately, virtuous capitalist behavior does not need to be artificially imposed by outside authority where it is lacking, because it can arise from normal competitive pressures. For that to happen, however, market competition must be allowed, and sometimes the widely accepted negative view of capitalism keeps this from happening.

Democracy suffers from the opposite image problem. After democracy came into being in large countries some 200 years ago, a remarkable dilemma emerged. On the one hand, democracy worked rather well: When compared to competing forms of government, democracy produced more humane, flexible, productive, and vigorous societies. It yielded responsive and able leaders (at least in comparison to most kings, czars, or dictators).

On the other hand, democracy hasn't come out looking the way many theorists imagined it could or should. It has been characterized by a great deal of unsightly and factionalized squabbling among self-interested, shortsighted groups. And most citizens seem disinclined to deliberate on politics the way idealists would like.

The Benefits of Capitalism

In modern America . . . we have automatic washing machines and clothes dryers (and inexpensive neighborhood laundries) that rescue us from the time-consuming, backbreaking, and dangerous labor of washing our clothes the pre-industrial way. When we need light, or want to listen to music or watch a movie, a flick of the wrist brings light instantaneously and a touch of a button brings expert performances to us in the privacy of our homes. When we wish to gossip with a friend 3,000 miles away, we do so effortlessly. Each of us bathes or showers whenever we want simply by turning on hot and cold running water from our taps. . . .

The fact is, material benefits enjoyed in the past only by the superrich are, in today's capitalist societies, enjoyed by nearly everyone. This undeniable fact demolishes accusations that capitalism creates inequality.

Donald J. Boudreaux, *Ideas on Liberty*, September 2002.

Theorists and reformers have generally responded to this with disappointment. Some conclude that democracy is just an attractive, impossible dream. Others try to refashion democratic institutions—and sometimes human nature—to approximate more nearly their rarefied theories. Democracy, urged John F. Kennedy, "requires the highest qualities of self-discipline, restraint, a willingness to make commitments and sacrifices for the general interest, and it also requires knowledge."

These kinds of claims only result in a bigger mismatch between democracy's reputation and the realities of human nature. And the blame lies more with our ideals than with the facts of life.

Perfection Does Not Exist

The truth is, perfect democracy is an oxymoron, and the undisciplined, chaotic, and essentially unequal interplay of "special interests" is democracy's whole point. The inevitable contrast between democracy's rough-and-ready reality and the hopelessly idealized conception so sonorously promulgated by people like Kennedy only inspires the very cynicism that democracy idealists bemoan and profess to want to reduce. What purists like to dismiss as "politics as usual" is actually just real democracy in action.

Ralph's Pretty Good Grocery in Lake Wobegon, a Minnesota town invented by humorist Garrison Keillor, operates under the sensible, if rather unexhilarating, slogan: "If you can't find it at Ralph's, you can probably get along without it." Both democracy and capitalism have triumphed, despite their image problems, in large part because people have been persuaded to accept a version of Ralph's slogan: The systems don't supply everything, but if you can't get it with democracy and capitalism, you can probably get along without it.

It is possible to create a society in which order reigns supreme, where there is none of the disorienting "churn" that characterizes both capitalism and democracy. But bitter experience shows such a society comes at the cost of flexibility, responsiveness, intellectual growth, and individual freedom. It's therefore better, on balance, to get along without the blessings an orderly society can bring.

Likewise, capitalism requires toleration of a considerable amount of insecurity, risk, and uncertainty. It may be possible, at least in principle, to design an economy in which individual station, prices, employment, and essential provisioning are authoritatively controlled. We've learned, though, that that approach stifles the invigorating effects of economic liberty, leading to slower growth and significantly less wealth overall. Experience thus suggests it is better to get along without total economic security.

Freedom Is Unfair

Both capitalism and democracy leave individuals free to pursue their interests, recognizing that some will simply do better in the pursuit than others. Unequal results will often emerge—because people have different capabilities. For some persons, particularly for those who are inclined to overrate their own abilities, this condition is deeply unpleasant, even unbearable. They become resentful.

Inequality will sometimes also result just because people have different luck. Some individuals just happen to be in the right place at a crucial moment. Sometimes an ill-considered, even foolish, gamble just happens to pay off. In an important sense, then, freedom is notably unfair.

But democracy is perhaps worse than capitalism in this regard. Capitalism does not profess to make everyone equally wealthy. The beguiling notion that "all men are created equal," however, has often been taken to suggest that some sort of equal outcome is guaranteed. Democracy, then, might seem somewhat hypocritical.

Capitalism and democracy can't supply complete orderliness, certainty, equality, security, and fairness. They are thus only pretty good—in the Ralph's Grocery sense. The laid-back perspective of the folks at Ralph's Pretty Good Grocery isn't very exhilarating, but it nicely avoids the dangers of overpromising.

And compared to their respective images, capitalism and democracy are pretty good in opposite senses. Democracy compared to its image is merely pretty good. While capitalism compared to its image is actually pretty good.

Living with Human Flaws

I suggest that one test of a fundamentally sound social institution is whether it can function adequately without demanding that people rise above the ignorance and selfishness with which they have been so richly endowed by their Creator. To put it gently, human beings are a flawed bunch, so any institution that's going to be successful had better be able to work with human imperfections, rather than requiring that the race first be reformed into perfection.

We're very fortunate that democracy doesn't require

people to be good or noble, but merely to calculate what is best for them or their society, and then to act only if they happen to be so inclined. We are very fortunate that capitalism raises and transforms selfishness and acquisitiveness into higher purposes. Democracy and capitalism are about as romantic as, in Charlotte Bronte's phrase, Monday morning. But that is a good thing.

"As a religion, especially an unnamed one, [capitalism] is dangerous."

Capitalism Is Not Always Beneficial

David Hilfiker

David Hilfiker works as a physician with the inner-city poor as part of a small Christian community. In the following viewpoint Hilfiker examines the underlying assumptions of capitalism, arguing that such notions are morally questionable and ultimately harmful to society. In his opinion, capitalism as it is currently practiced promotes selfishness, undermines the dignity of work, and defines profit and wealth as the fundamental goal of human endeavors. Spiritual ethics, which emphasize sharing, community, and justice for the poor, would provide better guidance and create a truly healthy society, Hilfiker concludes.

As you read, consider the following questions:
1. According to Paul Samuelson, cited by the author, what are the five underlying assumptions of capitalism?
2. Why is Adam Smith's notion of the "invisible hand" inherently flawed, in the author's opinion?
3. In Hilfiker's view, in what way is the free-market system unjust?

David Hilfiker, "Naming Our Gods," *The Other Side*, July/August 1998.
Copyright © 1998 by *The Other Side*. Reproduced by permission.

Today, we have trouble understanding service, sharing, justice, and equality . . . because, over the last generation, we've unwittingly transformed capitalism into a religion. . . .

The assumptions underlying capitalism have become essential metaphors in our deepest thinking about our society and ourselves. Unawares, we've allowed the language of capitalism to shape our basic assumptions about our lives—not only economic, but also social, political, and spiritual.

An older edition of the basic college textbook *Economics*, authored by Paul Samuelson, names the five underlying assumptions of capitalism.

The Basic Assumptions of Capitalism

First, capitalism assumes the economic system works best if each person pursues his or her selfish good, that is, the greatest profit. In *The Wealth of Nations*, Adam Smith proclaimed the principle of the 'invisible hand': "Every individual, in pursuing only his own selfish good, [is] led as if by an invisible hand, to achieve the best good for all. . . ."

Second, the profit motive drives economics. The *only* basis for making economic decisions is what brings the greatest profit.

Third, in order to make economic decisions, everything must have a price, including human labor. "Money . . . provides the measuring rod of values."

Fourth, decisions about whom to produce things for are determined by supply and demand, by relative income. The distribution of goods and services, therefore, is determined by the distribution of private wealth.

Fifth, wealth is primarily private property. "'Capitalism' got its name because . . . capital or 'wealth' is primarily the private property of somebody—the capitalist." The output of a business (after market-determined wages are paid) belongs to the "owner" of the capital.

These assumptions may or may not be the best ones upon which to build an economic system. In fact, most modern economists recognize their weaknesses, and most Western economies are significantly modified forms of capitalism. I'd like to explore how these assumptions have invaded our basic ideological and spiritual framework, affecting us to the point where they have become our new religion.

Selfishness as a Goal?

It is worth, then, revisiting the principles laid out in the Samuelson text with a critical, contemporary eye. How might they have affected our spirits? How might we root ourselves again in biblical perspectives?

Take the first—Adam Smith's "invisible hand." In effect, Smith said that if we were steadfastly selfish in our economic decisions, the "invisible hand" would make of everyone's selfish decisions a tapestry that benefits us all. We have not only the permission but also the responsibility to look only after our own self-interest.

This is a breathtaking supposition! Against the moral basis of virtually every world religion, selfishness becomes the goal. To be sure, it's been conclusively demonstrated that this assumption has overwhelming power to increase economic production. But do we want to enshrine selfishness as a primary value by which we *live?*

But we have. Self-interest has become so basic that we can hardly think outside it. . . .

Today, pop psychology counsels us that self-interest is the necessary ground of good relationships. Only by "looking after number one," it argues, can we relate mutually to each other. I sometimes catch myself defending my work with poor people by pointing out how much I get out of it. That's true, of course, but why do I need to claim self-interest? Why is *love* or *justice* not an adequate excuse?

Yet how many of us really believe that selfishness is a virtue, or that the world really works better if we look only to our own best interest?

While Adam Smith's pursuit of self-interest may or may not make good economics, it shares no common ground with biblical ethics, which emphasize love, community, and justice for the poor.

The Profit Motive

What of the second assumption, that within the capitalist system the purpose of economic activity is profit? Monetary return becomes the guiding motive for economic activity: how much advertising to buy, how many widgets to make, whether to open a branch in Peoria, or whether to downsize a corporation.

But note how *profit* is defined. It does not include the wages of workers, from entry level positions to managers. Wages are paid before profit is calculated. The guiding principle for all economic activity, then, is to maximize returns for the "investors" (those who are wealthy enough to have assets to invest). Note that only those who put money into the system are considered investors; workers do not usually "invest" by working.

The difference between investing and gambling (that is, trying to get immense returns for minimal money) is not always clear, at least in the modern stock market. Gambling, of course, did not originate in capitalism; nor did Adam Smith encourage people to profit unfairly. But the concepts of capitalism have given a certain unconscious legitimacy to these attempts at easy money.

There is a powerful perception today that "getting something for nothing" is really the way the world works. What one receives has little to do with the sweat equity one puts in but rather with wealth and the right kind of "luck." This has seeped into every area of our society.

What Is the Purpose of Work?

Some workers have always received more than others for an hour of work time. To question this is a societal taboo. But in recent decades, the discrepancies have multiplied. Top athletes, entertainment stars, and CEOs are obvious examples. Yet in many instances, doctors, lawyers, accountants, and other professionals receive much more than can be attributed to their "work." Bill Gates's amassing a fortune of well over $10 billion in twenty-five years is seen as a positive example of American ingenuity and success rather than a warning of a horribly warped system.

This focus on profit, on earning money, has mushroomed beyond the sphere of economics to become central to our understanding of life itself. The purpose of work is to make money.

Activities that are not financially remunerative, even those essential to societal well-being, are not valued. Is teaching the next generation less important than curing their physical ills? In our society, high salaries indicate that the work of a physician has more prestige and value than that of an elementary-school teacher. In Finland, on the other hand, the two earn approximately the same and carry equal status. In our society, the care of children at home—probably the most important thing we do for our future as a society—has no monetary value and is hardly considered a productive way to spend one's life.

Capitalism Is Dysfunctional

Despite all the praise we hear for the capitalist system, it is not really efficient when it comes to providing for the material needs of all people in society. It also causes many social problems. It is actually a dysfunctional system. . . .

Corporations . . . are pillaging our natural wealth with no consideration given to the common good.

Take for example our forests, which are invaluable for the good of humankind. They purify our air, store water for gradual use, regulate the climate, control floods, store soil nutrients, are a haven for wildlife and are used for recreation.

Yet the forests are disappearing at a steady rate because they are used for fuel, paper, packaging and wood products . . . Millions of people worldwide are dying due to polluted air and water. The earth is warming, and as a result the ice caps are melting and storms are becoming more violent.

Very little of this is addressed by the ruling class because effective remedial action would adversely affect profits.

Alan Bradshaw, *New Unionist*, August 2003.

The biblical view, of course, is that money is only a minor part of the purpose of work. We work to provide for the basic needs of our families and ourselves. But we also work out of love for others, to express our creativity, to be fulfilled, to create a better environment for our community, and to make a more just world. (Many people are reduced to working for money in an economic system that offers them nothing more, but that is clearly a violation of the biblical order.) . . .

The Bible judges the acquisition of surplus wealth to be inordinately dangerous to one's soul. Jesus was explicit about the pitfalls of wealth. Yet within capitalism, the primary purpose of the individual is the acquisition of surplus wealth. The societal desperation resulting from hoarded wealth is everywhere obvious. Yet our society (including the church) continues to exalt the accumulation of vast wealth.

What began as an innocuous economic principle has quietly seeped into our consciousness to reshape our underlying assumptions about the purpose of work, the goal of creativity, and the nature of humanity. That people within a capitalist system are oriented toward money is not a coincidence—it is a fundamental.

Money as a Measuring Rod

The third assumption argues that everything must have a price, and that money is the measuring rod of value.

The mechanism used to allocate resources in the free-enterprise system is price. The question, in deciding whether to buy a new machine or hire new workers, is, "Which costs less?" To determine how much people value something, the statistician asks how much they would pay. In my own profession, medicine, cost-benefit economic analysis has become a primary way to choose among treatment options—even though it requires giving a dollar value to human life.

When the assumption that everything has a price filters into our value system, we find we must struggle to hang onto values that have no price tag. Building community (to say nothing of building the reign of God) has no dollar value, so the medical students I talk to have no foundation for thinking about a career working with the poor.

In such a system, the only way to mobilize social forces against poverty is to show how much money society would save by investing in poor neighborhoods, alternatives to prison, and preventative medical care. In other words, by a cost-benefit analysis of poverty.

Again, few of us *believe* that everything has a price tag. We know there is no way to calculate the value of having a family or doing meaningful work. Yet if we act on that obvious reality, we are considered hopeless idealists. . . .

Choosing Injustice

Samuelson's fourth assumption states that the distribution of goods and services is determined by the distribution of private wealth. Those who have more money get more things.

This assumption is so deeply embedded in our value system that it's hard to even argue. If I ask, for instance, why, when compared with suburban schools, schools in poor areas are in physical disrepair, poorly supplied and equipped, and have low compensation for their teachers, the response is, "Well, the people in the city can't afford anything better."

Or if I ask, "Why do the children come to school hungry?" I hear back, "Well, their parents can't afford to give them anything for breakfast." Even if we don't like the responses, most of us will nod our head as if we had been given an "answer." But we haven't. We've only been given a statement of values.

An essential principle of the free-market system, then, is actually a formulation of injustice. The rich get whatever they want; the poor get nothing.

Again, few of us really believe that the world should operate this way. Some of us might agree to distribute *luxuries* according to wealth, but does anyone believe that food, shelter, basic education, healthcare, or other necessities should be distributed according to private wealth? Nonetheless, we have established a society in which even those necessities are meted out mostly on the basis of how much money people have.

It is important to understand that we have *chosen* this. Neither modern capitalism nor economic imperative requires that necessities be distributed according to wealth. Today's "capitalistic" economic systems can easily be modified through taxation and wealth-transfer programs, such as Social Security, to provide necessities for all.

Yet belief in the *religion* of capitalism is so deeply embedded in us that we have even, in the last few years, taken steps to dismantle the few societal mechanisms for providing necessities to those who—for one reason or another—do not possess private wealth. There seems to be an almost religious zeal for ensuring that nothing is left to the sentimentality of those who would make the basic societal needs available to all.

We have, in practice, accepted the basic injustice of the world as at least inevitable, if not proper. We seem incapable of the outrage of the prophets. We have lost our capacity for protest, our capacity to see and hold up alternatives.

The Sacredness of Private Property

This brings us to Samuelson's fifth and final assumption: Wealth is primarily private property that the owner can dispose of as he or she wishes.

Nothing is more deeply established in our economic system, more enshrined in popular consciousness, than the sacredness of "private property." Capitalism, of course, is dependent on the notion that the wealth a person amasses belongs to him or her. Without "private property," one could not have a capitalist system, since people cannot invest what they do not own.

Yet this value has gone far deeper than our ownership of things. To take my profession, physicians no longer feel much responsibility to society, even though society invests heavily in the education of physicians. (The cost to society to educate one doctor is over $1 million.) Instead, they view their degrees as "theirs" and believe they are free to use them as they will.

The assumption of "private property," nestled into our very being, has eroded our consciousness of the ties that link us to family, community, nation, and world. *My* things, *my* education, *my* abilities, *my* ideas—they all belong to me. My possessions and I become an island, separated from everyone else's islands.

It is common to hear that older people or younger couples without children have joined forces to vote down taxes for education in their community. The money belongs to them, and they have the legal right to vote against educating the future generations. But do we want to grant anyone the moral right to secede from the community?

The Native American concept that no one owns the land is well known. That most of us have difficulty even imagining life under such a concept—despite the obvious ravages to the environment under private ownership—is a sign of how deeply we have accepted the notion of "private property.". . .

Another Way

Western society hungers for values deeper than those it has. Even people who do not call themselves spiritual sense that something is desperately askew.

At a moral level, they realize that it isn't right for homeless families to walk the streets of the richest nation on earth. They know that global warming is dangerous and destructive. They acknowledge that people have a responsibility to one another. . . .

The function of religion in the human community should be to call forth our best and highest selves. As an economic system, capitalism may or may not serve us well. As a religion, especially an unnamed one, it is disastrous.

We must recognize where we are. We must find in our spirits the willingness to follow another way. We must share what we have found.

"Faith and the values that flow from it were central to the founding of this country."

Religion Is Essential to America

Joe Lieberman

Religious faith profoundly influences American values, contends Joe Lieberman in the following viewpoint. He maintains that the principles shared by both religious and nonreligious citizens are rooted in the Judeo-Christian tradition and in the notion that all are created equal by God. In recent decades, however, morality has declined as religious values have been seemingly banished from the public square. While it is important to maintain church-state separation, Americans should be encouraged to engage in an inclusive dialogue about faith to help renew the nation's moral and cultural life, he concludes. Lieberman, an Orthodox Jew, is a Democratic senator from Connecticut. This viewpoint is excerpted from a speech he delivered at the University of Notre Dame on October 24, 2000.

As you read, consider the following questions:
1. What social problems reveal a decline in American morality, according to Lieberman?
2. What statements made by George Washington and John Adams reveal that they understood the necessity of religion in a free society, according to the author?
3. In Lieberman's opinion, how did religion change America for the better between the eighteenth and the twentieth centuries?

Joe Lieberman, "Vision for America: A Place for Faith," *Responsive Community*, vol. 11, Winter 2000–2001, pp. 41–48.

It's been told that when Cardinal Montini, later to become Pope Paul VI, visited Notre Dame in the early 1960s, Father Theodore Hesburgh showed him the foundation for the new library—designed to be the largest college library building in the world. When his Eminence asked how he had raised the money, Father Hesburgh answered: "We haven't . . . yet." When Cardinal Montini looked astonished, Father Hesburgh told the future Pope, "Cardinal, you've got to *have faith.*"

That, in a phrase, is the message I bring to you today. Faith and the values that flow from it were central to the founding of this country. They have always shaped and stirred our national conscience. And now, at this moment of moral uncertainty, I believe our best hope for rekindling the American spirit and renewing our common values is to have faith again. Not just in our hearts, but in our communities. Not just in our private places of worship, but in our public spaces of conversation. And not just in our separate beliefs, but in our common commitment to our common purposes as Americans.

American Values

That common purpose is what makes us a unique people. America is the first nation that was founded not just as a set of borders, but as a set of ideals—that we are all created equal by God, that we are all endowed by Our Creator with inalienable rights, that we should all be free to pursue our dreams and realize the potential God gave every one of us. Here in America, if you work hard and play by the rules, you should be able to go as far as your talents take you.

But we also recognize that there must be more to our mission than securing opportunity and prosperity. Our nation is only as strong as our values, and right now, despite our material abundance, there is a persistent sense of unease about our moral future. As people peer into the national looking glass, they do not like the reflection of our values they see— the continued breakdown of families, the coarsening of life, the pollution of our culture, the erosion of classroom discipline, and the explosions of gunfire in our schoolyards. . . .

For America to realize its aspirations and to build the

more perfect union the Founders envisioned, we as a nation must strengthen our moral foundation, because so many of the social problems I mentioned a moment ago are in essence moral problems. We in government can help, through leadership and laws that reflect and reinforce our values. . . . But we also know a hard truth—that there are real and substantial limits to what the president, Congress, governors, or town councils can do to change the moral climate of this country.

That is because in our democracy, where our first principle is freedom, government cannot and must not try to control all of our behavior. It cannot force us to love and honor our parents, to treat our neighbors with respect, to care for those in need. Nor can it nourish our souls or do the rudimentary work of teaching us right from wrong. Those jobs have been and always will be entrusted to our traditional transmitters of values—religion, the family, and the broad range of civic organizations that collectively form the supportive sinews of civil society.

The Need for Religion in a Free Society

This is something the Founders understood implicitly and wrote explicitly into the Declaration of Independence and the Constitution. They were men of profound faith and recognized as such the necessity of religion in a free society. So said Washington as he warned us never to "indulge the supposition that morality can be maintained without religion." And so said [John] Adams when he wrote, "Our Constitution was made only for a moral and religious people."

In making these points, Washington or Adams could not have been suggesting that personal morality was entirely dependent on religion, or that those who do not believe in God are inherently immoral or even unpatriotic. If history and personal experience teach us anything, it's that there are many nonreligious people who are good men and women, and plenty of religious people who are not.

Rather, what Washington and Adams were saying is that our ideals, the inviolability of our rights, and the mission of our republic were inextricably linked to our belief in God and a higher law. That is why Jefferson showed such deference to the "Supreme Judge" in his Declaration. And that is why Madison and others made religious freedom the first freedom in the Bill of Rights. They knew that our experiment in self-government was contingent on our faith in the Creator who endowed us with the inalienable rights to life, liberty, and the pursuit of happiness.

Religion and Social Justice

In a great irony, the "politically correct" movement defending the rights of women, minorities, and the environment often positions itself as an enemy of the Christian church when, in historical fact, the church has contributed the very underpinnings that make such a movement possible. Christianity brought an end to slavery, and its crusading fervor also fueled the early labor movement, women's suffrage, human-rights campaigns, and civil rights. According to Robert Bellah, "there has not been a major issue in the history of the United States on which religious bodies did not speak out, publicly and vociferously."

Philip Yancey, *Books & Culture*, January/February 1998.

They also knew that, in a democratic state with limited power, religion, while not the only source, was certainly a most powerful source of values and good behavior. The core of those original values—faith, family, and freedom, equal opportunity, respect for the basic dignity of human life, and tolerance for individual differences—clearly had their roots in the Judeo-Christian ethic of the Founders. But they were not, and are not, exclusive to any one religious denomination. In fact, over the years they evolved into an American civic religion—deistic, principled, purposeful, moral, public, and not least of all, inclusive—a civic religion that cemented our bonds as Americans for generations and made real the ideal of *E pluribus unum*, from many one.

Ambivalence and Ambiguity

In recent decades, however, that consensus has gradually and subtly deteriorated into ambivalence. We have not abandoned our individual belief in those first principles. But we have grown increasingly unwilling to embrace and act on them publicly and collectively, and our moral muscles have slowly but surely atrophied as a result. More and more people shrink from drawing bright lines and making moral judgments, which are critical to the functioning of a free society. Too often, our ambivalence has slipped into ambiguity.

Nowhere is our ambivalence more apparent, or more consequential, than when it comes to our faith itself. We are still arguably the most religiously observant people on earth and still share a near universal belief in God. But you wouldn't know it from our national public life today. The line between church and state is an important one and has always been hard for us to draw, but in recent years we have gone far beyond what the Framers ever imagined in separating the two. So much so that we have practically banished religious values and religious institutions from the public square and constructed a "discomfort zone" for even discussing our faith in public settings—ironically making religion one of the few remaining socially-acceptable targets of intolerance. . . .

A Spiritual Rebirth?

In order to move beyond our ambivalence, we must first rebuild our moral consensus. We must work through our differences and suspicions to find space for faith in our public life.

A good place to start is to remember that religion, beyond being a unifying force throughout our history, has long informed and strengthened our sense of purpose, and changed our country for the better. In the 18th century, the first Great Awakening put America on the road to independence and freedom and equality. In the 19th century, the Second Awakening gave birth to the abolitionist movement and made more real the promise of equal opportunity. In the early 20th century, a third religious awakening inspired great acts of justice and charity toward the poor and the exploited. And in the 1960s, religious leaders and religious values helped energize the modern civil rights movement.

In recent years, I believe, there have been clear signs of a new American awakening. I suspect that this one began in the hearts of millions of Americans who felt threatened by the vulgarity and violence in our society, and turned to religion as the best way to rebuild a wall of principle and purpose around themselves and their families. It is as if millions of modern men and women were hearing the ancient voice of the prophet Hosea saying, "Thou hast stumbled in thine iniquity. . . . Therefore, turn to thy God . . . keep mercy and justice."

Our challenge now is to think about how we can expand the current spiritual awakening so it not only inspires us individually and within our separate faith communities, but also renews and elevates the moral and cultural life of our nation. The Catholic theologian Michael Novak has thought about this, and wisely advised: "Americans are starved for good conversations about important matters of the human spirit. In Victorian England, religious devotion was not a forbidden topic of conversation, sex was. In America today, the inhibitions are reversed." We must talk more to each other about our beliefs and our values, talking in the ecumenical spirit that unites us as a people, so that we may strengthen our common understanding and strengthen each other in our common quest.

An Inclusive Vision

That is a central part of our moral challenge: to answer the growing moral ambivalence with an open and inclusive vision of our common values, to show those who are of two moral minds that we are in fact one America. Through our dialogue, we must seize the opportunity and meet our responsibility to reach out to those who may neither believe nor observe, to reassure them that we share the same ideals with them, that our faith is not inconsistent with their freedom, and that our values do not make us disrespectful of their differences.

Discussion is only the beginning, because we know that in the end we will be judged by our behavior. In the Koran, the Prophet says: "So woe to the praying ones who are unmindful of their prayer—and refrain from acts of kindness." Isaiah summarizes the Torah in two acts: "Keep justice and do righteousness." And the Beatitudes inspire and direct us: "Blessed are they who hunger and thirst after righteousness for they shall be filled; blessed are the merciful for they shall obtain mercy. Blessed are the pure in heart for they shall see God. Blessed are the peacemakers for they will be called the children of God."

To make a difference, we must take our religious beliefs and values—our sense of justice, of right and wrong—into America's cultural and communal life.

> *"The U.S. Constitution is a secular document. It begins, 'We the people,' and contains no mention of 'God' or 'Christianity.'"*

Religion Is Not Essential to America

Dan Barker

In the following viewpoint Dan Barker maintains that America was founded on secular principles and not on a belief in God. Neither the Declaration of Independence nor the U.S. Constitution make any statements that endorse a specific religious faith, he points out. On the contrary, the United States became the first government in history to explicitly separate church and state. This church-state separation protects the rights of worshippers as well as nonbelievers, and it also ensures that America embraces diversity rather than theocracy, contends Barker. Formerly a Christian minister, Barker is now an atheist who writes a regular column for *Freethought Today*, a newspaper published by the Freedom from Religion Foundation.

As you read, consider the following questions:
1. According to the author, what did a 1797 treaty—written while George Washington was president—proclaim about America?
2. Under what circumstances did the phrase "separation between church and state" arise, according to Barker?
3. When did the phrase "In God We Trust" first appear on paper currency, according to Barker?

The U.S. Constitution is a secular document. It begins, "We the people," and contains no mention of "God" or "Christianity." Its only references to religion are exclusionary, such as, "no religious test shall ever be required as a qualification to any office or public trust" (Art. VI), and "Congress shall make no law respecting an establishment of religion, or prohibiting the free exercise thereof" (First Amendment). The presidential oath of office, the only oath detailed in the Constitution, does not contain the phrase "so help me God" or any requirement to swear on a bible (Art. II, Sec. 1, Clause 8). If we are a Christian nation, why doesn't our Constitution say so?

In 1797 America made a treaty with Tripoli, declaring that "the government of the United States is not, in any sense, founded on the Christian religion." This reassurance to Islam was written under Washington's presidency, and approved by the Senate under John Adams.

No Endorsement of Religion

What about the Declaration of Independence?

We are not governed by the Declaration. Its purpose was to "dissolve the political bands," not to set up a religious nation. Its authority was based on the idea that "governments are instituted among men, deriving their just powers from the consent of the governed," which is contrary to the biblical concept of rule by divine authority. It deals with laws, taxation, representation, war, immigration, and so on, never discussing religion at all.

The references to "Nature's God," "Creator," and "Divine Providence" in the Declaration do not endorse Christianity. Thomas Jefferson, its author, was a Deist, opposed to orthodox Christianity and the supernatural.

What about the Pilgrims and Puritans?

The first colony of English-speaking Europeans was Jamestown, settled in 1609 for trade, not religious freedom. Fewer than half of the 102 Mayflower passengers in 1620 were "Pilgrims" seeking religious freedom. The secular United States of America was formed more than a century and a half later. If tradition required us to return to the views of a few early settlers, why not adopt the polytheistic and natural beliefs of the Native Americans, the true founders of the continent at least 12,000 years earlier?

Most of the religious colonial governments excluded and persecuted those of the "wrong" faith. The framers of our Constitution in 1787 wanted no part of religious intolerance and bloodshed, wisely establishing the first government in history to separate church and state.

Church-State Separation

Do the words "separation of church and state" appear in the Constitution?

The phrase, "a wall of separation between church and state," was coined by President Thomas Jefferson in a carefully crafted letter to the Danbury Baptists in 1802, when they had asked him to explain the First Amendment. The Supreme Court, and lower courts, have used Jefferson's phrase repeatedly in major decisions upholding neutrality in matters of religion. The exact words "separation of church and state" do not appear in the Constitution; neither do "separation of powers," "interstate commerce," "right to privacy," and other phrases describing well-established constitutional principles.

What does "separation of church and state" mean?

Thomas Jefferson, explaining the phrase to the Danbury Baptists, said, "the legitimate powers of government reach actions only, and not opinions." Personal religious views are just that: personal. Our government has no right to promulgate religion or to interfere with private beliefs.

The Supreme Court has forged a three-part "Lemon test" (*Lemon v. Kurtzman*, 1971) to determine if a law is permissible under the First-Amendment religion clauses.

1. A law must have a secular purpose.
2. It must have a primary effect which neither advances nor inhibits religion.
3. It must avoid excessive entanglement of church and state.

The separation of church and state is a wonderful American principle supported not only by minorities, such as Jews, Moslems, and unbelievers, but applauded by most Protestant churches that recognize that it has allowed religion to flourish in this nation. It keeps the majority from pressuring the minority.

Upholding Minority Rights

What about majority rule?

America is one nation under a Constitution. Although the Constitution sets up a representative democracy, it specifically was amended with the Bill of Rights in 1791 to uphold individual and minority rights. On constitutional matters we do not have majority rule. For example, when the majority in certain localities voted to segregate blacks, this was declared illegal. The majority has no right to tyrannize the minority on matters such as race, gender, or religion.

Not only is it un-American for the government to promote religion, it is rude. Whenever a public official uses the office to advance religion, someone is offended. The wisest policy is one of neutrality.

Religion Can Be Dangerous

Neither belief nor nonbelief in a supernatural deity conduces automatically to goodness. Indeed, religion is very much a two-edged sword. It has been invoked to justify wars, crusades, hatred, the slaughter of dissenters, human sacrifice, terrorism, slavery, the subjugation of women and children, violations of human rights, the disparagement of sexuality, and today's disastrous overpopulation, among many other evils. It seems abundantly clear that, without foundational humanist values to mellow, guide, and restrain it, religion can become too dangerous to have around.

Robert F. Morse, *Free Inquiry*, Fall 2001.

Isn't removing religion from public places hostile to religion?

No one is deprived of worship in America. Tax-exempt churches and temples abound. The state has no say about private religious beliefs and practices, unless they endanger health or life. Our government represents all of the people, supported by dollars from a plurality of religious and non-religious taxpayers.

Some countries, such as the U.S.S.R., expressed hostility to religion. Others, such as Iran ("one nation under God"), have welded church and state. America wisely has taken the middle course—neither for nor against religion. Neutrality offends no one, and protects everyone.

The First Amendment deals with "Congress." Can't states make their own religious policies?

Under the "due process" clause of the 14th Amendment (ratified in 1868), the entire Bill of Rights applies to the states. No governor, mayor, sheriff, public school employee, or other public official may violate the human rights embodied in the Constitution. The government at all levels must respect the separation of church and state. Most state constitutions, in fact, contain language that is even stricter than the First Amendment, prohibiting the state from setting up a ministry, using tax dollars to promote religion, or interfering with freedom of conscience.

God and Secular Spaces

What about "One nation under God" and "In God We Trust?"

The words, "under God," did not appear in the Pledge of Allegiance until 1954, when Congress, under McCarthyism,[1] inserted them. Likewise, "In God We Trust" was absent from paper currency before 1956. It appeared on some coins earlier, as did other sundry phrases, such as "Mind Your Business." The original U.S. motto, chosen by John Adams, Benjamin Franklin, and Thomas Jefferson, is *E Pluribus Unum* ("Of Many, One"), celebrating plurality, not theocracy.

Isn't American law based on the Ten Commandments? Not at all! The first four Commandments are religious edicts having nothing to do with law or ethical behavior. Only three (homicide, theft, and perjury) are relevant to current American law, and have existed in cultures long before Moses. If Americans honored the commandment against "coveting," free enterprise would collapse! The Supreme Court has ruled that posting the Ten Commandments in public schools is unconstitutional.

---

1. During the 1950s, Senator Joseph McCarthy conducted a campaign to rid the U.S. government of Communists. McCarthy accused people without evidence and was eventually censured by Congress.

Our secular laws, based on the human principle of "justice for all," provide protection against crimes, and our civil government enforces them through a secular criminal justice system.

Why be concerned about the separation of church and state?

Ignoring history, law, and fairness, many fanatics are working vigorously to turn America into a Christian nation. Fundamentalist Protestants and right-wing Catholics would impose their narrow morality on the rest of us, resisting women's rights, freedom for religious minorities and unbelievers, gay and lesbian rights, and civil rights for all. History shows us that only harm comes of uniting church and state.

America has never been a Christian nation. We are a free nation. Anne Gaylor, president of the Freedom From Religion Foundation, points out: "There can be no religious freedom without the freedom to dissent."

Periodical Bibliography

The following articles have been selected to supplement the diverse views presented in this chapter.

Clark D. Adams	"My Cup Is Half Full: Why I Am Optimistic About the Rights of Nonbelievers," *Freethought Today*, October 2002.
Donald J. Boudreaux	"Equality and Capitalism," *Ideas on Liberty*, September 2002.
Lawrence W. Britt	"Fascism Anyone?" *Free Inquiry*, Spring 2003.
John Buell	"Patriotism, Democracy, and Dissent," *Progressive Populist*, November 15, 2001.
Forrest Church	"The American Creed," *Nation*, September 16, 2002.
Ruth Conniff	"Patriot Games," *Progressive*, January 2002.
Dinesh D'Souza	"What's So Great About America?" *American Enterprise*, April/May 2002.
Amitai Etzioni et al.	"What We're Fighting For: A Letter from America," *Responsive Community*, Fall 2002.
Gary Glenn and John Stack	"America: Fundamentally Religious," *World & I*, December 1999.
Paul Krugman	"For Richer: How the Permissive Capitalism of the Boom Destroyed American Equality," *New York Times Magazine*, October 20, 2002.
Ronald Radosh, interviewed by Stephen Goode	"Historian Takes a Political U-Turn," *Insight*, December 17, 2002.
Arthur M. Schlesinger Jr.	"A Question of Power," *American Prospect*, April 23, 2001.
James B. Twitchell	"It's a Material World, and That's OK," *Wilson Quarterly*, Spring 1999.
Anne Wortham	"America's Cultural-Institutional Core," *World & I*, November 2001.

CHAPTER 2

Is America in Moral Decline?

Chapter Preface

In examining American values, observers often point to popular culture as a measure of the nation's moral health. Many commentators, for example, argue that the amount of gratuitous sex and violence depicted in advertising, television, film, and popular music reflects America's moral and cultural decadence. Some contend, moreover, that a decadent entertainment industry also influences society—especially young people—and contributes to an increase in ignorance, incivility, immorality, and violence in America. As columnist John Leo maintains, "TV executives claim they are just 'reflecting society,' but they are shaping it, as well, helping to mainstream the coarse, confrontational attitudes embedded in gutter talk."

Those who agree with Leo often espouse the theory that the creators of mass culture intend to undermine America's traditional values. By plying the public with a constant barrage of violence, sex, and hedonism, some experts argue, the entertainment industry purposely conditions Americans to tolerate immorality and abandon restraint. "Much of what passes for culture today is, in fact, anti-culture," contends analyst Don Eberty. "Its chief aim is to emancipate, not restrain; to give free reign to human appetite, not moderate it. The role of entertainment . . . is to challenge and stretch standards. 'Break the rules!' 'Have no fear!' 'Be yourself!' are the common themes within mainstream cultural programming, and they are designed to discredit traditional forms of authority."

But other cultural analysts discount the notion that promoters of popular culture seek to subvert American values. According to *Time* journalists Jeanne McDowell and Andrea Sachs, much of today's mass culture highlights America's strengths rather than its shortcomings. For example, in an examination of how the terrorist attacks of September 11, 2001, have changed the nation, these journalists note that "the same social changes we are seeing in real life—reconnecting with family, regaining respect for institutions and community, fleeing the rat race—were already rampant in books, in movies and especially on TV." Many of the highest-selling series and movies of the past decade, they point out, feature characters who value home and community. These shows also focus on such topics as sacrifice, family reconciliation, and the emptiness of materialism. "When it comes to changed priorities and renewed purpose, popular culture has been there [and] done that," write McDowell and Sachs. *Washington Post* columnist Geneva Overholser agrees, adding that America's popular culture should be judged by its finest—not its worst—representatives: "We focus on some foul-mouthed rapper as if he were the sum total of all that we do and think, look at and listen to—as if he were somehow more representative of our culture than Duke Ellington or Martha Graham or Alfred Hitchcock. . . . [We need to review] the good things going on culturally and socially."

As the above comments suggest, notable thinkers have come to no single conclusion about the state of popular culture and its effects on American morality. In the following chapter, authors present additional opinions on whether America is experiencing a moral decline.

*"The young [rely] on their own value
systems to the exclusion of traditional value
systems from their parents or otherwise."*

America's Youth Are in Moral Decline

James A. Lee

American students have largely rejected traditional moral
standards, argues James A. Lee in the following viewpoint.
Their abandonment of conventional values is the result of a
progressive educational system that developed under the influence of social scientist Margaret Mead, the author points
out. According to Lee, Mead encouraged teachers to help
children reject parental influences, embrace the values of
their peer group, and become "free spirits." Consequently,
many of today's youths ignore traditional values and embrace their own dangerously misguided codes of ethics. Lee
is an emeritus professor of management in the College of
Business at Ohio University.

As you read, consider the following questions:
1. According to Thomas Martin, cited by the author, what
   percentage of surveyed students admit that they have
   lied to their parents?
2. How did the philosopher Jean Jacques Rousseau view
   education, according to Lee?
3. According to Lee, what experimental school was used as
   a model for training American teachers?

James A. Lee, "Why Our Children Have Rejected Traditional Values," *St. Croix
Review*, vol. 32, December 1999, pp. 29–32. Copyright © 1999 by Religion and
Society. Reproduced by permission.

Amerian conservative columnist Phyllis Schlafly recently noted in one of her columns that the students at the Columbine High School,[1] where thirteen were killed, received bizarre hands-on instruction in killing, death, suicide, and contempt for human life. In one class the students produced (as assigned) self-acted-out videos that glorified bloody violence and murder. They also had Values Clarification course work in which students are taught to reject moral absolutes and produce their own value systems—including actual exercises in which they are asked to decide whom they will allow to live and whom they will kill in accordance with their *own* criteria that will be completely acceptable to the instructor, no matter what they are.

In [the *St. Croix*] journal for June 1999, Professor Thomas Martin noted that while about ninety percent of surveyed students admitted that they lied to their parents, about this percentage was quite satisfied with their own ethics and character. As noted by Martin, the questionnaire did not ask them if they *were ethical*, but asked if they were satisfied with their *own* ethics and character.

The Influence of Margaret Mead

The origins of American students' rejection of parental, traditional or absolute values goes back at least to the influence over the educational establishment of Margaret Mead, her mentors, and her followers sixty to seventy years ago. Margaret Mead herself contributed enormously to the persuasion that the teacher and the child's parents are natural enemies. Writing in *Progressive Education* in 1941, she identified American school children as victims facing a "moral dilemma" when entering school:

> Whether his parents were born abroad and came to this country as adults . . . or [were] born abroad and came to this country as children. . . [were] born in this country of foreign-born parents . . . or whether he is the descendent of a long line of Old American stock: In any case, his home and the standards of his home are different from the standards of the homes from which his schoolmates come. During his first

1. On April 20, 1999, two students killed twelve schoolmates and a teacher at this Colorado high school before killing themselves.

months in school and increasingly throughout his school experience, he comes to realize that his parents' way of doing things is regarded by his schoolmates as foreign, odd, low-grade, queer, faddish, old-fashioned, newfangled.

After some fifteen hundred words expanding on the lonely forsaken child with the weirdo parents, Mead then guides the teacher into the heroine role:

> There is need as never before for the schools to train their students to stand on their own feet and act in terms of their own standards. . . . Instead of developing in pupils a clear sense of identification with the group . . . the teachers have vacillated between various authoritarian positions. Too often the teacher has stood over (*sic*) against the class, branding its allegiance to group values as wrong, instead of trying to dignify those values into wider values. . . . If the teacher could take advantage of the one point where the child can accept her without failing to make the usual American transition from home standards to current age group standards, *she would be able to lead young people into wider social loyalties about which they need not feel guilty. . . . The child formula would then be: "I have got to reject my home in detail, because it is different from the standards of my age mates."* [italics added]

The Rejection of Parental Authority

Note that Mead urged teachers to help the students behave according to their own standards, as though students had a full set of standards already operational. Mead could not have foreseen the technological explosion in communications which was to enable American youths to share nationwide, and now worldwide, a set of their very own "standards." Mead and others like her never seriously questioned the origins of these children's self-invented standards of conscience except to declare them virtuous, and to say that if the parents had anything to do with their development and acquisition, they were suspect and warranted rejection.

If Margaret Mead had been a garden variety neurotic patient, I believe that her therapist would have labeled her hostility to parents as pathological. I have read her writings, and I am impressed by her ability to work in her view that American parents are very undesirable persons for America's young to associate with. Sooner or later she could bend almost any topic to permit expounding on the evils of American parental influence on the young, and then exhort teachers, counselors, and judges to help the children break away from parents to follow their own "free spirits.". . .

Jean Jacques Rousseau

The origins of the ideological platform of which one plank formed the basis for the progressive education movement likely was begun on a grand scale by Jean Jacques Rousseau. His very attractive, idealistic concept of "natural man" in his *Discourse on the Inequalities of Men* and his *Social Contract* greatly influenced educational leaders such as Horace Mann, John Dewey, Margaret Mead, and A.S. Neill (of Summerhill).

The Need for High Standards

Our problem is that many of today's teachers and parents absorbed the anti-authority, anti-excellence ideology of the '60s, and as a result often fail to inspire or direct the young authoritatively. "Instead of offering challenges and clearly defined goals, we prefer to let kids slide by, for fear that many won't choose to work toward those goals," says Pat Welsh, [a] teacher.

This approach claims to be compassionate, but in fact it robs all children . . . of the chance to excel. Only high standards, clear direction, and genuine achievement in the face of stiff demands will ever stretch children to their full human potential.

Karl Zinsmeister, *American Enterprise*, May/June 1997.

Rousseau maintained that human beings were essentially good and equal in the state of nature but were corrupted by the introduction of property, agriculture, science, and commerce. His didactic novel, *Emile*, stated his view that education is not the imparting of knowledge but the drawing out of what is already in the child. Anyone familiar with a biography of Rousseau and his own autobiographical *Confessions*, can see his philosophy as a monumental effort to rationalize his own quite miserable, undisciplined, and immoral life. He describes his boyhood character as indolent, irritable, unprincipled. He stole, lied, and played dirty tricks. He was discharged from all the many jobs he held except for those from which he simply walked away. Throughout his life he was in and out of difficulties as a result of his classic psychopathic personality. Psychopaths are characterized by clinicians and criminologists as doing pretty much what they want to do when they want to, irrespective of the rights of others. Psychopaths are incapable of forming interpersonal attachments, unable to feel guilt for their transgressions, incapable of dependability or assuming responsibility, and suffer from emotional poverty. Rousseau's ideal society then was one in which such people like himself could easily thrive. Rousseau did pretty much as he liked—engaging in voyeurism, exhibitionism, masturbation in public—whenever he felt like it. He fathered a number of illegitimate children and promptly had them put away into foundling asylums, yet he wrote in *Emile*, "He who cannot fulfill the duties of a father has no right to become such."

Rousseau's great talent was in his brilliant persuasive writings in which he totally rejected the "civilization" of the eighteenth century. He saw schooling as a device to be used to help human beings in their natural revolt against civilization. He believed that mankind became corrupted in civilization in proportion to improvements in the arts and sciences. And his writing about how the world "should be" made him the idealist's idealist.

Summerhill

The first school of any note that was modeled after Rousseau's educational ideas was Summerhill, opened by A.S. Neill in 1921 in England. Neill's 1960 book, *Summerhill: A Radical Approach to Child Rearing*, was required reading in at least six hundred U.S. university courses in 1970, selling over two hundred thousand copies in 1969 alone. Here are a few quotes from the book:

The aim of education is to work joyfully and find happiness.

Make the school fit the child.

Lessons are optional. Children can go to them or stay away from them—for years if they want to.

The absence of fear is the finest thing that can happen to a child.

Heterosexual play in childhood is the royal road to a healthy, balanced sex life.

Rousseau's followers have used A.S. Neill's school as a basis for indoctrinating hundreds of thousands of American school teachers in their required courses in educational philosophy. This indoctrination rarely took into account the specifications of Neill's school. His student body numbered only forty to forty-five, with a teaching staff of seven. None of his students was from a poor family, and most were from atheistic families and above average in intelligence. In a society like America, which tries to educate everyone, rich or poor, a student-teacher ratio of six to one is hardly practical. In a society in which most parents are not atheists, such an approach to morals is bound to produce a further breach between parents and the school, especially with the help of educational philosophers like Horace Mann, Margaret Mead, John Dewey, *et al.*, persuading teachers to widen the breach whenever they can. . . .

In summary, the young's reliance on their own value systems to the exclusion of traditional value systems from their parents or otherwise, ought not surprise anyone who has reviewed the sixty years of pervasive influence of the educational establishment—persuading them to ignore all but their own "standards," consciences, morals, of codes of ethics. The recent movement to prop up their unearned self-esteem has allowed many of them to feel good about any sort of value system or code of ethics they choose to embrace as their very own.

"Maybe the Echo Boom [the current young generation] is big enough that the thousands of little things they do right will change society for the better."

America's Youth Are Advancing Morally

Jonathan V. Last

The youth of today exhibit a refreshing sense of morality, writes Jonathan V. Last in the following viewpoint. Today's teens are more likely to interact socially with their parents, avoid sex and drugs, and enjoy wholesome forms of popular entertainment, Last contends. While contemporary youths have not fallen prey to the vices that plagued previous generations, they are being raised with a weak sense of values and therefore lack a deep understanding of why morality is necessary. Their desire to do the right thing, however, may be all that is needed to create a healthier society, the author concludes. Last is a reporter for the *Weekly Standard*, a conservative journal of opinion.

As you read, consider the following questions:
1. In what way does "The Block" exemplify an improvement in teenage social life, according to Last?
2. In the author's opinion, what were the baby boomers notorious for?
3. According to Last, how does the popular culture of Generation X differ from that of the Echo Boom?

Jonathan V. Last, "Doesn't Smell Like Teen Spirit," *Weekly Standard*, vol. 4, February 15, 1999, pp. 22–25. Copyright © 1999 by News Corporation, Weekly Standard. All rights reserved. Reproduced by permission.

S ally, blonde, 15, and totally cool, minds her own business as she skates around the various ramps, cliffs, and cement obstacles that constitute the Vans Skate Park. Her gesticulating father, complete with backpack and video camera, bellows from the balcony of the parents' gallery, trying to get her attention. He finally catches her eye and—just as all the angst and embarrassment an A-list teenager feels towards her parents should come bubbling to the surface—she smiles and waves. Beaming, Sally skates over toward the balcony. Over the din of music her father shouts instructions about when to meet for dinner. And then, as they say good-bye, she blows him a kiss. At Vans, which may well be the epicenter of contemporary cool, rebellion is deader than Dillinger.[1]

Vans Skate Park is the cornerstone of America's newest outdoor mega-mall, The Block at Orange, an 811,909 square foot Mecca in suburban Los Angeles. Unlike other malls, most of which are 75 percent retail and 25 percent entertainment, The Block is about 75 percent entertainment and 25 percent retail. Jim Mance, the regional general manager for the Mills Corporation, which owns The Block, bridles at the term "mall." "This is really an entertainment center," he explains.

While the typical mall brings together stores like Nordstrom, Macy's, Hecht's, and Sears, The Block has Vans, a Ron Jon Surf Shop, a Virgin Megastore, Hilo Hattie ("the Store of Hawaii"), the two arcade/restaurants Dave & Buster's and Sega GameWorks, and a thirty-screen cineplex. Decorated in a style that can only be described as Disney in Vegas, the whole thing seems to be made of neon and glass. Along the open-air promenades stand "totems," some ninety feet high, which feature images of community role models. There is music all around, provided by hidden speakers that are controlled by a high-tech system of sensors that monitors noise levels throughout the mall and adjusts the volume of music accordingly. And like the monumental theme casinos of Las Vegas, every shop is an event unto itself, beginning with Ron Jon, which features a forty-foot high blue and

---

1. John Dillinger was a Depression-era bank robber who came to be seen as a "folk hero" outlaw.

aqua plastic wave as its storefront.

But the really astonishing thing about The Block is the behavior of the teenagers who pulse through it. Kids are smiling and laughing, mothers and daughters walk the promenade hand in hand, and no one looks the least bit alienated. Kids at The Block don't dress up, but they wear what can be described as high casual. The girls walk around in jeans that flare politely at the knee and fitted tops in bright, cheery colors like violet, sky blue, taupe, and red. The boys wear khaki cargo shorts and loose white or slate-blue T-shirts. Everyone wears Skechers, the hottest name in footwear.

And there aren't many couples at The Block. Except for the occasional mixed group, boys and girls travel in separate packs, which often include—gulp—parents.

A Better Teen Social Life

As suburban sprawl became the norm in America, the center of teenage social life moved from Main Street to the mall. Built for adults, these shopping centers were soon overrun by teens. Malls were places where smoking and fighting were the rule and where unsupervised kids ran amok. The quintessential teen movie of the 1980s, *Fast Times at Ridgemont High*, rightly taught America to expect a large degree of surliness and revolt from kids in malls.

The Block rewrites that lesson almost completely. Kids here don't smoke or curse. Very few have body piercings. Warning signs caution against "unnecessary staring," "the non-commercial use of laserpointers," and "engaging in non-commercial expressive activity without proper written permission." One rule requires skateboarders carry their boards when they are not at Vans. And that is exactly what they do.

The Block was built specifically for *teens and their parents*. This marketing combination would have seemed impossible only a decade ago. But now, it appears, parents have returned to adolescent upbringing in ways that have rendered their children's normally destructive impulses mute. In turn, teenagers' hangouts have undergone a change, as evidenced by The Block, and their pastimes have taken a turn for the better.

Skateboarding, for example, used to be the domain of rebels. It was a non-sport sport—an athletic activity with no organization, and hence no concept of team or competition—that was performed illicitly in parking garages and town squares. Skateboarding's lack of conformity—key to teenagers with visions of Holden Caulfield[2] buzzing in their brains—made it the pastime of outlaws, the bad seeds who went behind school during lunch to sneak cigarettes. Now, Vans has legitimized skateboarding, making it sociable and about as rebellious as soccer.

Parents and Kids Together

The Vans complex looks like a personal-injury attorney's version of heaven. It is filled with ramps, ledges, and steep drop offs onto hard, unforgiving cement. There are two large empty in-ground pools and a professional-size half pipe. The skateboarders are not devil-may-care scofflaws, but smiling Stepford-like adolescents, each wearing—as required—a helmet and knee and elbow pads. Parents watch from a gallery that rings the complex, some basking in the ebullience of their progeny, while others sit comfortably on the blue plastic bleachers and leaf through the *Orange County Register*. When one 16-year-old boy accidentally runs down a smaller skateboarder, there is no glaring, no harsh words. He hops off his board and runs back to help the other boy up, apologizing profusely. The two of them laugh and then go their separate ways.

When their skate session ends at Vans, lots of boys head directly to Sega GameWorks, a theme arcade that is a joint venture between video-game giant Sega and the movie studio DreamWorks SKG. Unlike the dark, sweaty arcades the Sean Penn character Jeff Spicoli haunts in *Fast Times*, Game-Works is a bright, spacious place with the latest virtual-reality games. It even has a restaurant where adults can wait while their kids go skiing, racing, rafting, or even fishing. The video games at GameWorks run on debit cards that can be bought with adult-sized $20, $30, $40, or $50 credits. The other mega-arcade, Dave & Buster's, is so family friendly that all kids must be accompanied by an adult.

And while the boys are out being boys, the girls behave

2. Holden Caulfield is the central character in J.D. Salinger's *The Catcher in the Rye*.

surprisingly girlishly. The Block offers a number of places for mothers and daughters to bond, including Old Navy, the no-frills alternative to the Gap and Eddie Bauer. At Ultrahouse, the popular home furnishings store for teenagers, pairs of mothers and daughters coo over lava lamps. Ultrahouse is the source of all things translucent and inflatable, including chairs, loveseats, pillows, picture frames, and even Christmas trees. It is the perfect place for Boomer mothers to teach their teenage daughters the nuances of nesting. And, after a healthy bit of shopping, they're off to see a tear jerker such as *Patch Adams* on one of the thirty screens at the AMC multiplex.

The Generosity of Today's Youth

There is a great deal of simple goodheartedness, instinctive fair-mindedness, and spontaneous generosity of spirit in our young people. . . . They form wonderful friendships, they seem to be considerate of and grateful to their parents—more than baby boomers were. (In many ways contemporary young people are more likable than the baby boomers—less fascinated with themselves, more able to laugh at themselves.) An astonishing number of them are doing volunteer work. . . . They are donating blood to the Red Cross in record numbers, they deliver food to housebound elderly people. They spend part of their summer vacation working with deaf children or doing volunteer work in Mexico. This is a generation of kids that, with relatively little guidance and religious training, is doing some very concrete and effective things for other people.

Christina Hoff Sommers, *St. Croix Review*, June 1998.

When all the consumption becomes too much, parents visit Starbucks while their kids retreat to Jamba Juice, where they eagerly plunk down $3.95 to recharge with drinks like the Kiwi-Berry Burner—a "Power Smoothie" that comes with a "juice boost" in Vita, Protein, Immunity, Fiber, Femme, or Energy flavors. If you've ever watched television or seen the pictures of dejected, slacker teens on the covers of *Newsweek* or *Time*, it's enough to make you wonder who these kids are.

From Baby Boom to Echo Boom

To understand today's teenagers, you first have to understand American demographic history since the Second World War.

In 1945 the men who had fought returned home to peace and prosperity and produced the largest number of children ever born in a single generation. The 76.8 million babies born between 1946 and 1964 were famously called the Baby Boomers, a cohort notorious for their selfishness and narcissism. The first generation to champion abortion and divorce, they were plagued first by drug use and then by mercenary careerism. As the Boomers began to settle down, they had children later in life than any other generation, and so between 1965 and 1978, only 52.4 million children were born. This shadow generation, called Generation X, was defined by the anti-child sentiments that racked their parents and created the "latch-key kid." Boomer parents helped produce, among other unsavory things, a generational malaise in the lives of their first born.

But the Boomers weren't bad, just spoiled and slow to learn. By the time the younger ones got around to having children, they started to get parenting right and the result is a second wave—an "Echo Boom"—of children, some 77.6 million of them born after 1979. Suddenly the radicals who marched for unrestricted access to abortion were sheepishly admitting that they wanted it to be only "safe, legal, and rare." The protest junkies who made chemical living mod became terrified that their kids might try marijuana. Working mothers were replaced by soccer moms. And the new economic prosperity allowed the younger Boomers to dote on their kids almost as fully as their parents had on them. As a result, the differences between Generation X and their younger cousins couldn't be more striking.

The Change in Popular Culture

Consider the popular culture. Every generation has a crossover genre of music that makes a splash into the mainstream. In the '50s it was rock, in the '60s it was folk, in the '70s it was disco, and in the '80s it was hard-core rap and *Smells Like Teen Spirit*–style grunge. Today's hit crossover genre is country. Where Gen X embraced the nihilism of N.W.A. and Ice-T, the Echo Boom adores the wholesome Shania Twain, the Dixie Chicks, and Garth Brooks. (Faith Hill, the aptly named country singer, played at the opening of The Block.) Where the popular '80s industrial anthem *Head Like a Hole* from Nine Inch Nails cried, "Head like a hole / black as your soul / I'd rather die / than give you control," today's teens adore the bubble-gum pop sounds of Barenaked Ladies and Jewel, who begins her hit song *Hands* with, "If I could tell the world just one thing / it would be / we're all ok."

Gen X dressed in ripped jeans and dark, sullen, earthy tones, while the Echo Boom chooses neat styles and bright colors. Even kids' bodies have changed: Whereas Gen X celebrated the thin, frail, torpor of heroin chic, nearly all the kids at The Block still have a healthy smidgen of baby fat.

The statistics bear out the change. The Centers for Disease Control reports that since 1991, the percentage of teens who have never had sex has risen 11 percent. More than half of all boys and girls in high school now graduate without having sex. In their new book, *The Ambitious Generation*, Barbara Schneider and David Stevenson cite survey data that show, in contrast to teens in the '70s and '80s, almost half of today's teens "feel appreciated for who they are" and think of their parents as "emotionally supportive." Drug use is down, and after a decade of Gen Xers being despondent about their prospects for fulfillment, survey after survey shows teens exuberantly optimistic about their futures.

The Shadow of Moral Relativism

To hope that these changes in behavior lead to a generational moral reformation is probably unrealistic. A recent issue of *Teen People* featured a special section on religion where the editors presented the views of five teens, a Methodist, a Jew, a Buddhist, a Muslim, and an agnostic, making each seem a pleasant novelty. And so religion is with teenagers, because while teens seem to know that there are things that should be done—abstention from sex, avoidance of drugs—they don't quite know why. They can articulate the reasoning behind right-minded popular morality, like saving the environment or fighting drunk driving, but they don't have a vocabulary for explaining more serious things. For all the attention their parents have lavished on them, today's teenagers were raised in the shadow of moral relativism. Whatever the merits of the Boomers' reformation, they still don't have the gumption to look their children in the eye and declare that they were wrong to live the way they once did—just as they can't bring themselves to condemn President [Bill] Clinton for sins they too have committed. And so the Echo Boom is growing up without a moral compass: doing the right things, but guided only by the warm reassurances of pop psychology and the innate desire to avoid the mistakes of their elders.

In that sense, it seems futile to hope that the Echo Boom will embark on a quest to make right all of the problems their parents created in the culture. But maybe they don't need to. Size does matter, and maybe morality is as morality does. In the same way that it makes no difference whether Deep Blue, the IBM computer that beat Gary Kasparov in chess, "thinks" its way to victory or simply makes the necessary calculations to get there, maybe it's all right for teens to do the right thing in service to the inarticulate ethos of New Age living.

Boomers devastated American morality not by one great centrally-planned blow, but by a thousand individual cuts, each a service to self-centered hedonism. What made society conform to them, however, was their demographic mass, not their generational character. Maybe the Echo Boom is big enough that the thousands of little things they do right will change society for the better every bit as much as the Boomers changed it for the worse.

But that argument is for another day. Today, we should just be grateful that Sally and her dad get along, which, seen in the dim light of the Gen X world, is no small miracle in itself.

*"So many, under the influence of the
entertainment media, have largely
abandoned morality and self-restraint."*

Popular Culture Undermines
American Values

Steve Bonta

American values are being subverted by modern mass entertainment, argues Steve Bonta in the following viewpoint.
The constant barrage of violence, sex, hedonism, and other
forms of decadence in today's popular culture is conditioning
Americans to tolerate immoral attitudes and conduct, he contends. Moreover, writes Bonta, the creators of today's entertainment media actually intend to destroy traditional values
by plying the public with titillating sensory images that produce involuntary responses. The entertainment industry is
therefore a threat to freedom because it persuades people to
embrace vice and immorality, Bonta asserts. Bonta is a writer
for the *New American*, a conservative biweekly journal.

As you read, consider the following questions:
1. What kind of a place is Aldous Huxley's "brave new
   world," according to the author?
2. What is the "Mass Man," in Bonta's view?
3. In Bonta's opinion, how can Americans escape the effects
   of media-promoted immorality?

Steve Bonta, "Bread and Circuses," *New American*, vol. 19, February 10, 2003,
p. 28.

The Roman satirist Juvenal, writing in the first century AD, lamented that "the people that once bestowed commands, consulships, legions, and all else, now meddles no more and longs eagerly for just two things—bread and circuses." Juvenal had the misfortune of living in a time when the civic virtues of the early Roman republic were a distant memory, when the moral dry rot, which eventually destroyed Rome from within, was already far advanced. Juvenal saw that the Roman citizenry had become so addicted to entertainment and pleasure that they had lost the capability of governing themselves. Juvenal's scornful term "panem et circenses"—bread and circuses—has become synonymous with mindless self-gratification.

Closer to our own time, novelist and futurist Aldous Huxley foresaw a "brave new world" where religious and moral restraints have been completely abandoned, in which the masses are kept in a permanent stupor with recreational drugs, carnal pleasures, and mindless entertainment. Huxley's novel is not so well known or gracefully written as [George] Orwell's *1984*. But with the benefit of decades of hindsight, we would do well to ponder whether Huxley's predictions, and not Orwell's, were closer to the mark.

What Huxley understood more acutely than Orwell is that it is easier to enslave a people by seduction than by coercion. In the words of social critic Neil Postman, "what Orwell feared were those who would ban books. What Huxley feared was that there would be no reason to ban a book, for there would be no one who wanted to read one. . . . As Huxley remarked . . . , the civil libertarians and rationalists who are ever on the alert to oppose tyranny 'failed to take into account man's almost infinite appetite for distractions.' In *1984*, Huxley added, people are controlled by inflicting pain. In *Brave New World*, they are controlled by inflicting pleasure."

From Thought to Thoughtless Stupor

In the past century, mass entertainment has become our defining cultural trope. With the advent of television, radio, cinema, phonographs, and, more recently, CDs and the Internet, we passed from a culture of the written word to a culture of the visual and aural electronic image. The shift has been subtle but devastating. We no longer rely on written texts to transmit ideas, but on pictures and sounds. As an unavoidable result, we have become conditioned to the use of sensory images rather than reasoned, verbal discourse characteristic of what Postman called the "Typographic Age." We base our opinions and value judgments, therefore, not on reason, but on sensory impressions and the emotions they trigger.

It is difficult for modern man to comprehend the vast gulf between what liberal historian Henry Steele Commager dubbed the "Empire of Reason"—that is, 18th and 19th century America—and the United States at the beginning of the 21st century. Early America was a society of words, when attention spans were (for us moderns) incomprehensibly long, and the ability to grasp complex clause structures and sophisticated reasoning was taken for granted among the elite and the middle class alike. Who today can imagine enduring the format of the Lincoln-Douglas debates of the mid-19th century, when the candidates sparred for hours at a time, and were typically allotted an hour or more apiece to make opening statements? How many educated Americans today would be comfortable reading and discussing the likes of Blackstone and Plutarch, which early educated Americans were nearly as familiar with as the Bible? Finally, how many modern Americans would tolerate the following sample of late 18th-century political discourse, even if it were served up under klieg lights on network TV, and delivered by an impeccably groomed politician:

> Knowledge is in every country the surest basis of public happiness. . . . To the security of a free Constitution it contributes in various ways: by convincing those who are entrusted with the public administration, that every valuable end of government is best answered by the enlightened confidence of the people; and by teaching the people themselves to know, and to value their own rights; to discern and provide against invasions of them; to distinguish between oppression and the necessary exercise of lawful authority . . . [and] to discriminate the spirit of liberty from that of licentiousness, cherishing the first, avoiding the last, and uniting a speedy, but temperate vigilance against encroachments, with an inviolable respect to the laws.

Those words formed part of George Washington's very

first State of the Union address, a comparatively brief but exquisitely worded gem of political thought. Washington was primarily concerned with the precious principles of liberty, in this case, the importance of knowledge and education to maintaining a free republic. In stark contrast, consider George W. Bush's take on the same subject, in his first State of the Union address given in January 2001:

> The highest percentage increase in our budget should go to our children's education. . . . [E]ducation is my top priority and, by supporting this budget, you'll make it yours, as well.

> Reading is the foundation of all learning. So during the next five years, we triple spending, adding $5 billion to help every child in America learn to read. Values are important, so we've tripled funding for character education to teach our children not only reading and writing, but right from wrong. . . . When it comes to our schools, dollars alone do not always make the difference. Funding is important, and so is reform. So we must tie funding to higher standards and accountability for results. . . . Children should be tested on basic reading and math skills every year between grades three and eight. Measuring is the only way to know whether all our children are learning. And I want to know, because I refuse to leave any child behind in America.

In President Bush's simple, patronizing prose and shallow materialist cant we recognize all the hallmarks of modern political discourse. Government leaders today, like President Bush, seem both unwilling and unable to discuss any issue deeper than spending taxpayer dollars on the latest nanny-state proposal.

Manipulative Mass Media

What has so degraded our ability to reason and to communicate ideas (and not just about government) in the more than two centuries between the founding era and the present? Simply put, modern mass entertainment. Commented Postman:

> Las Vegas is a city entirely devoted to the idea of entertainment, and as such proclaims the spirit of a culture in which all public discourse increasingly takes the form of entertainment. Our politics, religion, news, athletics, education and commerce have been transformed into congenial adjuncts of show business, largely without protest or even much popular

notice. The result is that we are a people on the verge of amusing ourselves to death.

There is, of course, nothing wrong with entertainment per se. Good music, movies, and other forms of entertainment can enrich and give balance to our lives. Unfortunately, we have become addicted not only to entertainment for its own sake, but also to modes of entertainment that debase our morals and degrade our intelligence. Many Americans have become like the citizens of Huxley's dystopia, who dissipated their energies in mindless games like Centrifugal Bumblepuppy and amoral, sensuous diversions like the feelies and the orgy-porgy. Too many of us tolerate and even welcome into our homes "entertainment" whose sole purpose is to titillate and debase. From Ozzie and Harriet Nelson we have descended to Ozzy and Sharon Osbourne, whose heavy-metal lifestyle is now held up as a model for emulation. From the smooth lyrics and refined rhythms of the crooners and the Big Bands, we've moved to the shouted obscenities and buzz-saw instrumentals of modern rap and heavy metal. And since the demise of Hollywood's oft-maligned production code, we are now served mostly mindless erotica and computer-enhanced mayhem masquerading as cinema.

The Goals of Hollywood

Hollywood appears unwilling to change its program of subjecting the American public to greater amounts of sex, drugs, and violence—falsely claiming that this is what America wants. But Hollywood's output is not a true reflection of America's moral climate; it is a reflection of what the cultural subverters hope America will become. Today's youth, especially, are facing an immense struggle against an industry seeking to define, manipulate and condition them with explicit images of depravity, hopelessness, and mindless diversion—with the grand design that younger generations will eventually be manipulated into accepting socialist remedies.

Jennifer A. Gritt, *New American*, October 23, 2000.

The mandarins of mass entertainment have a revolutionary agenda, and their methods aren't hard to understand. They intend to destroy traditional Western culture, religion, and morals by using the power of the modern entertainment media. They know, and have known for decades, that sensory images are far more effective than words for mass manipulation because they have the power to elicit an involuntary response. Images force themselves on our minds whether we like it or not; it is impossible to see a violent image or an erotic picture and not react, however fleetingly. Thus, when we hear racy songs, see suggestive billboards and TV ads, or watch television shows with morally subversive themes and bawdy content, we are unavoidably being conditioned to tolerate and, eventually, embrace vice, that "monster of so fearful mien, as to be feared needs but to be seen" that Alexander Pope warned of.

With its base enticements, our modern mass entertainment media are every would-be revolutionary's fondest dream. In the first place, modern electronic media conveniently encourage us to communicate, and to interpret ideas, in terms of sensory images rather than in words. As a result, popular opinion has confused the rapid-fire, media-produced images—which permeate our lives, constantly seeking to arouse us—with more traditional modes of communication, like speech. This is why inane claims seeking to elevate pornographic pictures and obscene song lyrics to the level of First Amendment–protected "free speech" are so widely accepted.

The Mass Man

Moreover, the mass media have helped to create the Mass Man, in philosopher Jacques Ellul's pungent terminology. The modern Mass Man is an utter conformist who goes along to get along. He identifies with the crowd—a generation, ethnic group, or what have you—accepting and retailing its slogans, reveling in conformity and content with ignorance. The Mass Man is nothing new; he is merely the participant in the mobs of ancient Greece and revolutionary France, amplified by the mesmerizing power of modern mass entertainment. His habitat is the rock concert, the campus demonstration, the sports arena, or anywhere that he can be titillated by the adrenalin surge of mass participation.

It's impossible to shut out mass entertainment entirely. Even if we eliminate television and the Internet from our homes, we still hear the obscene bawling of the latest top 40 bands in most public places. We still see the pornographic front covers of popular magazines on display at the grocery checkout counter. We can't escape the billboards, the media-anointed superstars, and the teenagers with their tee-shirts bearing the alphanumeric names of the latest rap stars. We are fast approaching the society of omnipresent entertainment and universal indulgence that Huxley depicted.

Entertainment as a propaganda vehicle is often far more effective than more traditional modes of indoctrination, such as dis-information disguised as news broadcasts. This is partly because people tend to lower their guard when presented with material marketed as entertaining or aesthetically satisfying, rather than informative. America's entertainment industry has propagandized on behalf of morally and politically subversive themes for decades. As producer David Victor, whose projects included TV medical dramas like *Marcus Welby, M.D.* and *Dr. Kildare*, once boasted: "With varying success we did the story of homosexual rape, an unwed father, unwed mothers, abortions, drug addiction, indecent exposure. . . . I'm proud of that. I think I educate as well as entertain.". . .

A Threat to Freedom

Little wonder that, after decades of having pro-abortion, pro-homosexuality, pro-sexual promiscuity, and anti-religion messages, among others, dinned into them on prime-time TV, in movies, and in popular music, Americans have largely acquiesced, and in many cases openly embraced, conduct and beliefs that were taboo a couple of generations ago.

Because of its power, because of its omnipresence, and above all, because of its depravity, modern mass entertainment is one of the greatest threats to our freedom that we have ever faced. We are dangerously close to losing the ability to sustain free republican government, because so many, under the influence of the entertainment media, have largely abandoned morality and self-restraint. The newly minted age of the Internet has hastened the process, by giving virtually every home ready access to pornography, that basest of all entertainment, with its devastating influences.

Ben Franklin warned that "only a virtuous people are capable of freedom. As nations become more corrupt and vicious, they have more need of masters." Great republics die like aging trees, from the inside out. By the time of Juvenal, Rome was at the height of her imperial splendor, seen from the outside. But within, the Rome that had produced men like Cicero and Scipio was already gone. The hollow shell of empire persisted for centuries thereafter, but its demise had already been largely determined, because the Roman citizenry had come to prefer diversion over virtue. . . .

The Empire of Reason

We would do well to rediscover the Empire of Reason, if we are to place ourselves beyond the deadening influence of venal popular entertainment. The best personal antidote for mindless rock 'n' roll is cultivating an active interest in classical and other forms of elevating music. The best defense against the smog of propaganda-as-entertainment is immersion in the great books of the past. And the surest way to escape the rip tide of media-promoted immorality is to recommit ourselves to the moral virtues and family values of a more civilized age, an age that may yet be revived if we do not entertain ourselves into oblivion.

"[Popular culture] does no great harm."

Popular Culture Does Not Undermine American Values

John Derbyshire

In the viewpoint that follows, John Derbyshire maintains that contemporary popular culture has no significant effect on American values. While he grants that much of today's popular entertainment is mindless and vulgar, he does not believe that it seriously influences individual personality development or society's moral trends. Furthermore, Derbyshire concludes, it is important to safeguard liberty by protecting freedom of expression—censoring distasteful images and ideas should not be allowed. Derbyshire is a contributing editor of the *National Review*, a journal of conservative opinion.

As you read, consider the following questions:

1. According to Derbyshire, what are the three possible policy positions concerning sex and violence in the entertainment media?
2. What is the author's view on children's exposure to fictional violence?
3. What is the current "price to be paid for liberty," in Derbyshire's opinion?

John Derbyshire, "First Amendment First: Why Hollywood Should be Left Alone," *National Review*, vol. 52, no. 9, October 9, 2000. Copyright © 2000 by National Review, Inc., 215 Lexington Ave., New York, NY 10016. Reproduced by permission.

O n September 9, [2000], we had our annual block party in my suburban, lower-middle-class street. The event's centerpiece was a talent show, the brainchild of our 10-year-old neighbor Siobhan. She herself performed three songs: "It Was Our Day," from the group B*Witched, and the Britney Spears numbers "What U See (Is What U Get)" and "Lucky."

For readers not au courant with the pop-music scene, the first of these songs is a mawkish elegy for a dead friend: "Heaven, heaven was calling you/ Heaven, heaven needed you/I'll lay a rose beside you for ever." The second is a girl's protest against her boyfriend's possessiveness: "I know you watch me when I'm dancin'/When I party with my friends/I can feel your eyes on my back, baby/I can't have no chains around me." The third is about the inner loneliness of a Hollywood star. "She's so lucky, she's a star/But she cry, cry, cries in her lonely heart."

So there I was, sitting on a plastic chair on my neighbor's lawn, watching a 10-year-old girl singing about grief, sexual jealousy, and the hollowness of success. As I squirmed, I sank into reflections of the curmudgeonly kind: Is this all kids know nowadays? There used to be innocent songs that preteens could sing—can remember a hundred of them: "Green Grow the Rushes-O" and so on. Now there are no topics, for anyone of any age, but sex and death.

"It's the Culture"

Miss Spears had been in the newspapers that very morning; at the MTV Music Video Awards two nights before, 18-year-old Britney had taken off everything but a few strategic spangles and performed the kind of dance for which lonely men in soiled raincoats used to pay extravagant door charges to ill-lit basement clubs. If I were to tell you that I switched the thing off in disgust I should be guilty of a falsehood; but I am awfully glad my daughter Nellie (a 7-year-old whose contribution to the talent show was a faultless performance of Dvorak's "Humoresque" on violin) didn't see it. Yet even she already knows some Britney lyrics. They all do, preteens and pre-preteens. As parents say with a sigh, when you bring this up: It's the culture.

The culture came up often over the next few days. The following Monday the FTC [Federal Trade Commission] released its report on the marketing of violence in the media. Meanwhile, the Senate Commerce Committee was holding hearings on the issue. Lynne Cheney showed up to urge show business to police itself, and to quote some lyrics from hip-hop star Eminem, who had won a major award at the MTV bash. One of Eminem's songs expresses the satisfaction a man feels at having raped and murdered his mother. Joe Lieberman went further before the committee, urging the FTC to step in and regulate media companies who would not tone down their products. Al Gore, on his way from one showbiz fund-raiser ($800,000) to another ($6.5 million), agreed.

Policy Possibilities

What to make of all this? So far as public policy is concerned, there are three possible positions, identified here by those who take them.

My neighbors: It doesn't matter much, so there's no point getting steamed. As an influence on the development of my children, my words and my example outweigh by a factor of hundreds anything Britney Spears does.

Mrs. Cheney: The media companies that promote creatures like Eminem should be shamed before the public, and thereby persuaded to mend their ways. Gore-Lieberman and their trial-lawyer pals: Legislate, regulate, intimidate. Sure, there'll be some grumbling from Hollywood; but they will never defect to the party of the dreaded "Christian Right."

Most conservatives would sympathize with Mrs. Cheney; I greatly admire her myself. If, however, my neighbors are representative of the larger American public, as they probably are, then her program is a non-starter. We must therefore choose between the first of the above options and the third. Can there be any doubt which poses the greater threat to our ancient liberties?

Entertainment and Character

What we are talking about here, remember, is sex and violence. The second of these gives me no trouble. I have never had much patience with the idea that children should be shielded from fictional violence. I would much rather my own children discover *The Hunchback of Notre Dame* as I did, in the thrilling sado-necrophiliac original, shot through with cruelty and lust, than via the lathe jollity of the Disney version. Here I can appeal to the wisdom of great storytellers from the past, who spared children very little. Check out the original "Cinderella," in which the ugly sisters get their eyes pecked out. Children take this stuff in their stride. They may even, as Bruno Bettelheim argued, be helped by it. Certainly the evidence that exposure to graphic violence causes violent deeds is highly suspect: "Shooting the Messenger," a recent report by the Media Coalition (available on their website), persuasively refutes the kiddie-see, kiddie-do arguments.

Does Media Violence Cause Societal Violence?

Would the incidence of violence, sex and intoxication seriously diminish if those topics disappeared from our screens? This seems to be the apple-pie view of most psychologists. . . . But it is not a point that has been proved. . . .

Professor Jonathan Freedman at the department of psychology at the University of Toronto . . . concluded that "there is little convincing evidence that in natural settings viewing television violence causes people to be more aggressive." In 1992, he wrote that "research has not produced the kind of strong, reliable consistent results that we usually require to accept an effect as proved. It may be that watching violent programs causes increased aggressiveness but, from a scientific point of view, this has not been demonstrated."

Ben J. Wattenberg, *Values Matter Most: How Republicans or Democrats or a Third Party Can Win and Renew the American Way of Life.* New York: Free Press, 1995.

Sex is more worrisome. As the doting father of little Nellie, I naturally spend a lot of time fretting about this. How will the vulgarity of our public entertainment shape her personality?

Our September 9 block party came on the anniversary of Elvis Presley's first appearance on *The Ed Sullivan Show* [more than forty] years ago. The following January, Sullivan had Elvis on for the third time; it was then that he issued his famous order for the singer to be shown only from the waist up, in order that younger viewers might not be inflamed by the sight of his hip movements. We have traveled an awfully long way from Ed Sullivan to the MTV awards show. What is really surprising, though, is how little harm has been done.

It needs some effort of imagination now to recall the alarm that Elvis raised at that time. Frank Sinatra called Elvis's music "the most brutal, ugly, desperate, vicious form of expression it has been my misfortune to hear." This comment reflected a widespread public attitude.

If, in 1956, you had asked any thoughtful American what consequences might follow from the abandonment of all customary restraint in entertainment, and from related phenomena like the attempted normalization of homosexuality, he would probably have said that the Republic could not survive such a transformation. Plainly these good people believed something that was, in fact, untrue: that the stability of society depended on the exclusion, by common consent, of certain things from the sphere of public display.

No Great Harm

The insouciance of my neighbors in the face of today's popular culture is, therefore, quite sensible. It's the culture—but it doesn't matter; it does no great harm.

To be sure, much mayhem has passed before our eyes since 1956. We have gone through Francis Fukuyama's "great disruption" with all its attendant phenomena: soaring rates of crime, bastardy, divorce, and so on. But we have come through to the other side at last; as Fukuyama himself points out, the indicators are trending downwards now, toward "re-normalization." And in all that happened, which was cause and which effect? Did Elvis—or Madonna, or Howard Stern—have one-thousandth the influence on our culture that (say) the Pill had?

The world changes. As a conservative, I shall conserve what I can; but if I am to keep any influence over my children at all, some measured degree of acceptance is called for. There is a price to be paid for liberty, and Eminem and Britney Spears are the current coin in which that price must be paid. They will not be shamed, and they ought not be banned: for if the guardians of our public virtue can outlaw hip-hop lyrics, you can be sure that "hate speech" will be their next target, and it is all too easy to imagine where that will lead. With the Second Amendment swirling down the drain, the survival of the First can no longer be taken for granted.

"Consumerism as a creed means we must keep upping the ante. Enough is never enough, and soon we are possessed by our possessions."

Consumerism Harms American Culture

Dolores Curran

Consumerism has become the guiding principle in America's capitalist society, argues Dolores Curran in the following viewpoint. Americans are programmed to believe that buying things will bring them happiness and fulfillment, so they often become caught up in a never-ending pursuit of material satisfaction. The hunger for more and more possessions creates unhealthy levels of individualism and competitiveness that alienate people from each other, the author maintains. True happiness is found not in acquisitions, but in spirituality, religious faith, loyalty to causes, and love for one another, Curran concludes. Curran is an author and expert on parenting and family issues who lives in Littleton, Colorado.

As you read, consider the following questions:
1. What traits do healthy families possess, in Curran's opinion?
2. According to John Kavanaugh, cited by the author, what is the "catechetics of capitalism"?
3. According to Curran, what do people do when they are spiritually impoverished?

Dolores Curran, "There Is a Lot to Be Said for Less," *U.S. Catholic*, vol. 64, February 1999, p. 14. Copyright © 1999 by Claretian Publications. All rights reserved. Reproduced by permission.

A djacent cars parked outside a supermarket boasted an intriguing pair of bumper stickers. The one on the left proclaimed, "I shop. Therefore, I am." The one on the right responded, "Been there. Done that." These messages sum up the promise and disillusionment of subscribing to a cultural creed that equates happiness and meaning with possessions and pleasures.

The Religion of Capitalism

Consumerism has been called the religion of capitalism. Even our federal government supports the notion by labeling families "consumer units." From earliest childhood, we are bombarded with messages to buy items we don't need and don't have time to enjoy, messages that promise pleasure, fulfillment, and social acceptance. Children are taught that they should want Furbies, Beanie Babies, Giga Pets, or Tickle Me Elmo dolls for Christmas because they are designated popular toys for a given season, and parents feel obligated to buy them so the child's self-esteem and social standing won't suffer.

Inside the supermarket, alongside the usual bank of shopping carts, we find miniature carts for children bearing poles with the sign "Customer in Training." No surprise that by the time we reach adolescence we are inculturated into believing that the good life is measured more by what we have than by who we are. As we age, we refer to our new cars, computers, and other acquisitions as toys; we buy into the conventional wisdom that we are what we drive, compute, and wear. Then we wait impatiently for the elusive happiness promised.

We are well-programmed to believe in consumerism as the panacea to happiness, the antidote to emptiness, and the entitlement of hard work. It takes a strong person to resist this creed, a countercultural person. Those who choose voluntary simplicity as an alternative way of life report that they are regarded as odd, underachieving, and even unpatriotic by friends and family who constantly yearn and work for more goods and pleasures to give meaning to their lives.

In my research on families, I have found that healthy families possess a strong religious core, but it doesn't always mean a strong church affiliation. Rather, it indicates that the family finds its meaning in something other than consumerism: in faith in God, in love for one another, in service to others, in righting injustice, in a cause or movement, or in sharing goods and hospitality.

When a family has no deeper reason for being, pleasure becomes the meaning and purpose of life. When the pleasure in an object or experience wanes, a new object for happiness must be identified. Together, the family saves and works to obtain it, which provides a sense of bonding, but once the new item is acquired and the novelty wears off, the family needs to identify another, and the cycle repeats itself. Jesuit Father John Kavanaugh calls this the "catechetics of capitalism."

Never Enough

We often try to solve our problems by buying. A mother in one of my parenting groups made this startling statement: "We aren't getting along very well in our family so we're thinking of getting a camper van." When questioned, she admitted she had bought into the advertising promise that camping creates happy families, although deep down she knew they would simply take their family problems along with them.

The problem of consumerism as a creed means we must keep upping the ante. Enough is never enough, and soon we are possessed by our possessions. Shopping is the number one cultural activity in America. Accumulation of unnecessary goods has become a habit—even an addiction—as we wring our hands over lack of storage space. What we once considered luxuries we come to regard as necessities, and eventually we become dependent upon the things we acquire.

Consumerism as a way of life demands competition, workaholism, and individualism. When we're bent on acquiring a bigger home, more cars, season tickets, and the latest computers, we work longer hours and spend less time with those we claim to love. For job security and promotion, we compete with fellow workers rather than cooperate with them. It's each person for him- or herself. Dog-eat-dog.

"I can love my neighbor. No sweat," one man said. "But

don't tell me to love or help the man in the workplace who's eyeing my job."

How do we reconcile our consumer creed with Christianity? With great difficulty. Jesus does not equivocate when he warns us about the tyranny of possessions: "Take care to guard against all greed, for though one may be rich, one's life does not consist of possessions."

STAR OF BETHLEHEM

Kirk. © by Kirk Anderson. Reproduced by permission.

Jesus goes on to tell the story of the rich man who kept building bigger barns (today's wail: "I need more storage space"), and he ends the passage with: "But God said to him, 'You fool, this night your life will be demanded of you; and the things you have prepared, to whom will they belong?'" And Jesus concluded, "Thus will it be for the one who stores up treasure for himself but is not rich in what matters to God" (Luke 12:15–21).

Counter the Culture

Consumerism as such is neither negative nor sinful. It's how we regard it and what it replaces that brings it into conflict with our professed beliefs. In his encyclical Centesimus annus, Pope John Paul II says, "It is not wrong to want to live better; what is wrong is a style of life which is presumed to be better when it is directed toward 'having' rather than 'being,' and which wants to have more, not in order to be more but in order to spend life in enjoyment as an end in itself."

He touches upon the greatest cost of cultural consumerism: It is embraced to fill an emptiness that can only be filled by a loving relationship with God. When this spiritual relationship is attained, we no longer need to search for things to give life meaning or make us happy. We live in a quiet joy of inner peace that no object can supply. Further, this oneness with God extends to those around us. We shine as expressions of God's love to others, a love that reflects upon us and increases our joy.

Mother Teresa noted that although the people she cared for were economically impoverished, she found Americans spiritually impoverished by substituting the "good life" for the Christian life of simplicity, sharing, and caring for one another in love. When we are spiritually impoverished, we try to fill the void with such things as education, work, food, sex, travel, sports, and shopping. Like drugs, these activities numb the emptiness at first, but God is a relentless nag who refuses to allow shallow pleasures to fulfill our hunger for him.

Eventually we become disillusioned with the futility of acquiring more and "I shop. Therefore, I am" degenerates to "Been there. Done that." It's a grace-filled moment, this revelation of the betrayal of consumerism. Kavanaugh writes, "Having faced the dominant gospel of our culture and compared it to the gospel of Christ, we should arrive at a growing recognition that our relation to this culture can be only as people apart. . . . Persons still yearn to live lives of integrity. They yet yearn for mystery that is not magical but personal. Service still beckons them. They feel the suffocation of a closed materialistic universe, and their pain surfaces in a variety of searches for something and someone beyond."

And who is that someone beyond? The one we call our Father, who loves us so dearly that he wants us to live in joy, not cheap gratification. He sent his son to teach us that we are a people apart. Our very Baptism signifies that we are countercultural because we aspire to higher values than wealth, possessions, power, and prestige.

Where Treasure Is Found

A huge gap exists between the creeds of the cultural consumer and the Christian consumer. The cultural consumer lives by—and is betrayed by—bumper-sticker messages, advertising promises, and a constant search for pleasure. The Christian consumer lives by the word of the Lord, "Do not lay up for yourselves an earthly treasure. . . . Remember, where your treasure is, there your heart is also."

We are the People of God who profess to care for and share our riches with those who are economically impoverished. Saint Ambrose said, "You are not making a gift to the poor man from your possessions but you are returning what is his." When we understand these words and opt for simple living, loving, giving, and the inner peace that comes only from a deep intimacy with God, we are no longer enslaved by consumerism. We are no longer spiritually impoverished. Then we are free to proclaim, "I believe. Therefore, I am."

"The triumph of consumerism is the triumph of the popular will."

Consumerism Benefits American Culture

James B. Twitchell

James B. Twitchell, a professor of English and advertising at the University of Florida, writes in the following viewpoint that consumerism is the driving cultural force in America and in much of the world today. Although consumerism does have its drawbacks, most people want to have access to a variety of material goods, and commercial culture is a necessary part of mankind's social evolution. Furthermore, Twitchell maintains, the process of consumption can be both pleasurable and meaningful. Consumerist culture ultimately creates a more egalitarian and democratic world, he contends. Twitchell is the author of *Lead Us into Temptation: The Triumph of American Materialism.*

As you read, consider the following questions:
1. According to Twitchell, how does the academic establishment tend to view consumerism?
2. What are some of the drawbacks of consumerism, in the author's view?
3. What will the globalization of capitalism lead to, in Twitchell's opinion?

James B. Twitchell, "In Praise of Consumerism," *Reason*, vol. 32, August 2000. Copyright © 2000 by the Reason Foundation, 3415 S. Sepulveda Blvd., Suite 400, Los Angeles, CA 90034. www.reason.com. Reproduced by permission.

Sell them their dreams. Sell them what they longed for and hoped for and almost despaired of having. Sell them hats by splashing sunlight across them. Sell them dreams—dreams of country clubs and proms and visions of what might happen if only. After all, people don't buy things to have things. They buy things to work for them. They buy hope—hope of what your merchandise will do for them. Sell them this hope and you won't have to worry about selling them goods.

—Helen Landon Cass

Those words were spoken some years ago by a female radio announcer to a convention of salesmen in Philadelphia. The *Philadelphia Retail Ledger* for June 6, 1923, recorded Ms. Cass' invocations with no surrounding explanation. They were simply noted as a matter of record, not as a startling insight.

There are two ways to read her spiel. You can read it like a melancholy Marxist and see the barely veiled indictment of the selling process. What does she think consumers are—dopes to be duped? What is she selling? Snake oil?

Or you can read it like an unrepentant capitalist and see the connection between consuming goods and gathering meaning. The reason producers splash magical promise over their goods is because consumers demand it. Consumers are not sold a bill of goods; they insist on it. Snake oil to the cynic is often holy water to the eager. What looks like exploiting desire may be fulfilling desire. . . .

The Academic View of Consumerism

I think that much of our current refusal to consider the liberating role of consumption is the result of who has been doing the describing. Since the 1960s, the primary "readers" of the commercial "text" have been the well-tended and -tenured members of the academy. For any number of reasons—the most obvious being their low levels of disposable income, average age, and gender, and the fact that these critics are selling a competing product, high-cult (which is also coated with its own dream values)—the academy has casually passed off as "hegemonic brainwashing" what seems to me, at least, a self-evident truth about human nature: We like having stuff.

In place of the obvious, they have substituted an interpretation that they themselves often call vulgar Marxism. It is supposedly vulgar in the sense that it is not as sophisticated as the real stuff, but it has enough spin on it to be more appropriately called Marxism lite. Go into almost any cultural studies course in this country and you will hear the condemnation of consumerism expounded: What we see in the marketplace is the result of the manipulation of the many for the profit of the few. Consumers are led around by the nose. We live in a squirrel cage. Left alone we would read Wordsworth, eat lots of salad, and have meetings to discuss Really Important Subjects.

In cultural studies today, everything is oppression and we are all victims. In macrocosmic form, the oppression is economic—the "free" market. In microcosmic form, oppression is media—your "free" TV. Here, in the jargon of this downmarket Marxism, is how the system works: The manipulators, a.k.a. "the culture industry," attempt to enlarge their hegemony by establishing their ideological base in the hearts and pocketbooks of a weak and demoralized populace. Left alone, we would never desire things (ugh!). They have made us materialistic. But for them, we would be spiritual. . . .

The Triumph of Stuff

The idea that consumerism creates artificial desires rests on a wistful ignorance of history and human nature, on the hazy, romantic feeling that there existed some halcyon era of noble savages with purely natural needs. Once fed and sheltered, our needs have always been cultural, not natural. Until there is some other system to codify and satisfy those needs and yearnings, capitalism—and the culture it carries with it—will continue not just to thrive but to triumph.

In the way we live now, it is simply impossible to consume objects without consuming meaning. Meaning is pumped and drawn everywhere throughout the modern commercial world, into the farthest reaches of space and into the smallest divisions of time. Commercialism is the water we all swim in, the air we breathe, our sunlight and shade. Currents of desire flow around objects like smoke in a wind tunnel. . . .

This isn't to say that I'm simply sanguine about such a material culture. It has many problems that I have glossed over.

Consumerism is wasteful, it is devoid of otherworldly concerns, it lives for today and celebrates the body. It overindulges and spoils the young with impossible promises. It encourages recklessness, living beyond one's means, gambling. Consumer culture is always new, always without a past. Like religion, which it has displaced, it afflicts the comfortable and comforts the afflicted. It is heedless of the truly poor who cannot gain access to the loop of meaningful information that is carried through its ceaseless exchanges. It is a one-dimensional world, a wafer-thin world, a world low on significance and high on glitz, a world without yesterdays.

The Truth About Materialism

Look at the pathetic offerings of the anti-materialists, the limp "anti" philosophy of lines like "Money can't buy love" and "Money can't buy happiness." Lies we tell on the way to the mall.

We ought to just own up to the truth: Wealth may not buy love, but it's a much better come-on than poverty. We can admit that wealth buys admiration, attention, mates.

And while money can't buy happiness, it can buy pleasures, and as long as you're stringing together new and better pleasures, you're happy.

Dale Dauten, *St. Louis Post-Dispatch*, November 24, 1997.

On a personal level, I struggle daily to keep it at bay. For instance, I am offended by billboards (how do they externalize costs?); I fight to keep Chris Whittle's Channel One TV and all place-based advertising from entering the classroom; political advertising makes me sick, especially the last-minute negative ads; I contribute to PBS in hopes they will stop slipping down the slope of commercialism (although I know better); I am annoyed that Coke has bought all the "pouring rights" at my school and is now trying to do the same to the world; I think it's bad enough that the state now sponsors gambling, do they also have to support deceptive advertising about it?; I despise the way that amateur athletics has become a venue for shoe companies (why not just replace the football with the Nike swoosh and be done with it?); and I just go nuts at Christmas.

Understanding Commercial Culture

But I also realize that while you don't have to like it, it doesn't hurt to understand it and our part in it. We have not been led astray. Henry Luce was not far off when he claimed in a February 1941 editorial in *Life* magazine that the next era was to be the American Century: "The Greeks, the Romans, the English and the French had their eras, and now it was ours." Not only that, but we are likely to commandeer much of the 21st century as well.

Almost a decade ago, Francis Fukuyama, a State Department official, contended in his controversial essay (and later book) "The End of History?" that "the ineluctable spread of consumerist Western culture" presages "not just the end of the Cold War, or the passing of a particular period of postwar history, but the end of history as such: that is, the end point of mankind's ideological evolution". OK, such predictions are not new. "The End of History" (as we know it) and "the endpoint of mankind's ideological evolution" have been predicted before by philosophers. Hegel claimed it had already happened in 1806 when Napoleon embodied the ideals of the French Revolution, and Marx said the end was coming soon with world communism. What legitimizes this modern claim is that it is demonstrably true. For better or for worse, American commercial culture is well on its way to becoming world culture. The Soviets have fallen. Only quixotic French intellectuals and anxious Islamic fundamentalists are trying to stand up to it.

To some degree, the triumph of consumerism is the triumph of the popular will. You may not like what is manufactured, advertised, packaged, branded, and broadcast, but it is far closer to what most people want most of the time than at any other period of modern history. . . .

The Globalization of Capitalism

In a consumerist culture, the value-making ligatures that hold our world together come from such conventions as advertising, packaging, branding, fashion, and even shopping itself. It is a system presided over by marketers who deliver the goods and all that is carried in their wake. It is a more democratic world, a more egalitarian world, and, I think, a more interesting world.

That said, commercialism can be a stultifying system too, and wasteful. It would be nice to think that this eternally encouraging market will result in the cosmopolitanism envisioned by the Enlightenment philosophers, that a "universalism of goods" will end in a crescendo of hosannas. It would be nice to think that more and more of the poor and disenfranchised will find their ways into the cycle of increased affluence without contracting "affluenza," the "disease" of buying too much. It would be nice to think that materialism could be heroic, self-abnegating, and redemptive. It would be nice to think that greater material comforts will release us from racism, sexism, and ethnocentricism, and that the apocalypse will come as it did at the end of Shelley's *Prometheus Unbound*, leaving us "Sceptreless, free, uncircumscribed. . . . Equal, unclassed, tribeless, and nationless. . . . Pinnacled dim in the intense inane."

But it is more likely that the globalization of capitalism will result in the banalities of an ever-increasing, worldwide consumerist culture. Recall that Athens ceased to be a world power around 400 B.C., yet for the next three hundred years Greek culture was the culture of the world. The Age of European Exposition ended in the mid-20th century; the Age of American Markets—Yankee imperialism—is just starting to gather force. The French don't stand a chance. The Middle East is collapsing under the weight of dish antennas and Golden Arches. The untranscendent, repetitive, sensational, democratic, immediate, tribalizing, and unifying force of what Irving Kristol calls the American Imperium need not result in a Bronze Age of culture, however. In fact, who knows what this Pax Americana will result in? But it certainly will not produce what Shelley had in mind.

Our Better Judgment

We have been in the global marketplace a short time, and it is an often scary and melancholy place. A butterfly flapping its wings in China may not cause storm clouds over Miami, but a few lines of computer code written by some kid in Palo Alto may indeed change the lives of all the inhabitants of Shanghai.

More important, perhaps, we have not been led into this world of material closeness against our better judgment. For many of us, especially when young, consumerism is not against our better judgment. It is our better judgment. And this is true regardless of class or culture. We have not just asked to go this way, we have demanded. Now most of the world is lining up, pushing and shoving, eager to elbow into the mall. Woe to the government or religion that says no.

Getting and spending have been the most passionate, and often the most imaginative, endeavors of modern life. We have done more than acknowledge that the good life starts with the material life, as the ancients did. We have made stuff the dominant prerequisite of organized society. Things "R" Us. Consumption has become production. While this is dreary and depressing to some, as doubtless it should be, it is liberating and democratic to many more.

Periodical Bibliography

The following articles have been selected to supplement the diverse views presented in this chapter.

Richard Alleva	"How Sick Can We Get?" *Commonweal*, July 13, 2001.
American Enterprise	"Liberal Parents, Lost Children," March 2002.
Holly Lyman Antolini	"Naming Our Demons?" *Witness*, April 1999.
Christian Century	"Moral Collapse?" March 10, 1999.
Paul Ekins	"From Consumption to Satisfaction," *Resurgence*, November/December 1998.
Kate Langrall Folb	"'Don't Touch That Dial!' TV as a— *What!?*—Positive Influence," *SIECUS Report*, June/July 2000.
Jennifer A. Gritt	"Hollywood's Subversive Agenda," *New American*, October 23, 2000.
John A. Howard	"Liberty and Responsibility," *St. Croix Review*, June 2000.
John Kavanaugh	"Beautiful Rottenness," *America*, April 2, 2001.
Jeanne McDowell and Andrea Sachs	"The Culture Comes Home . . . ," *Time*, November 19, 2001.
Leah McLaren	"Shopping Is Not Just for Christmas," *Spectator*, December 14, 2002.
Geneva Overholser	"American Culture—Give It a Break," *Washington Post National Weekly Edition*, February 16, 1999.
David C. Stolinsky	"Our Titanic Nonjudgmentalism," *New Oxford Review*, April 2000.
Robert Tracinski	"Hollywood's Moral Perspective," *Intellectual Activist*, April 2001.
David Whitman	"More Moral—America's Moral Non-Decline," *New Republic*, February 22, 1999.
Rebecca Wyatt	"Bought in the U.S.A.," *Insight on the News*, December 20, 1999.

CHAPTER 3

How Should Patriotism Be Defined?

Chapter Preface

After the terrorist attacks of September 11, 2001, Americans experienced a resurgence of patriotism. To revere those who had been killed, to honor firefighters, police, and rescue workers, and to express a sense of national belonging, people displayed American flags at their homes, on their vehicles, and on their clothing. "There's no doubt in my mind that it had something to do with the sudden realization of how fragile are our freedom and liberty, which we had taken for granted much too long," states journalist Charles S. Lauer. "The terror attacks, from people who hate our values and culture, showed us how vulnerable we are."

In the ensuing months, the Bush administration launched a "war on terror," a multifaceted strategy that included bombing campaigns in Afghanistan, new domestic security measures, and warfare against Saddam Hussein's regime in Iraq. According to most polls, a majority of Americans initially supported the administration's antiterrorism policies and believed that it was important to maintain a united front while the nation remained under the threat of attack. Bumper stickers and T-shirts proclaimed "United We Stand" and "God Bless America." American troops who were deployed to Afghanistan and Iraq were proudly hailed as selfless defenders of freedom—and as exemplars of great patriotism for their readiness to sacrifice their lives for American ideals and interests.

Yet many citizens disagreed with the Bush administration's approach to fighting terrorism—and this disagreement ignited heated debates concerning the definition of patriotism. Before the United States launched strikes against Iraq in March 2003, antiwar groups staged protests around the world. The numbers of participants were unprecedented—it was the first time in history that so many people had joined in such protests before a war had actually begun. Antiwar protesters in the United States, however, were greeted with mixed reactions, with many pundits and politicians openly questioning their patriotism. In a televised interview after an antiwar rally, Duncan Hunter, a Republican representative from San Diego, California, stated, "What [the protesters] are doing is really horrible. It actually borders on treason." An unidentified military wife, shown later on the same broadcast, agreed: "Our troops need to know that we are behind them 100 percent. These protesters could hurt our troops by damaging their resolve and their morale. I'm appalled at their hatred of America."

Sam Smith, editor of the *Progressive Review*, disagrees: "We justly pledge allegiance to the republic for which America stands, but we do not have to pledge allegiance to . . . failed policies for which America is now suffering. . . . If our country is about to run into the street without looking, there is absolutely nothing disloyal about crying 'Stop!' True patriotism is an act of love, not of hate." In the opinion of Smith and other Americans who question U.S. government policies, the right to political debate and dissent is a treasured liberty that a true patriot should exercise and defend, even during times of national crisis and war.

In the following chapter, several authors representing different points on the political spectrum continue this discussion on how patriotism is best defined and expressed.

"[Media and schools should] nourish and expand our imaginations by presenting non-American lives as deep, rich and compassion-worthy."

Valuing Diversity Is Patriotic

Martha C. Nussbaum

Martha C. Nussbaum is a professor of law and ethics at the University of Chicago and the author of several books, including Cultivating Humanity: A Classical Defense of Reform in Liberal Education. *In the following viewpoint Nussbaum maintains that patriotic feelings for one's country can easily degenerate into feelings of superiority and a desire to humiliate or defeat other nations. Such was the case for many Americans in the wake of the terrorist attacks of September 11, 2001, she argues. While a love of one's country is natural and necessary, Americans should find ways to extend empathy and compassion to people beyond their borders. Education could help expand the sympathy that Americans feel for their own people into a broader concern for human vulnerabilities in other nations, Nussbaum concludes.*

As you read, consider the following questions:

1. What specific incident does Nussbaum recount as an example of "us versus them" thinking?
2. According to Aristotle, cited by the author, what are the three components of compassion?
3. In Nussbaum's opinion, why should patriotism not be renounced?

In the aftermath of [the terrorist attacks of] September 11, [2001], we have all experienced strong emotions for our country: fear, outrage, grief, astonishment. Our media portray the disaster as a tragedy, that has happened to our nation and that is how we very naturally see it. So too the ensuing war: It is called "America's New War," and most news reports focus on the meaning of events for us and our nation. We think these events are important because they concern us—not just human lives, but American lives. In one way, the crisis has expanded our imaginations. We find ourselves feeling sympathy for many people who did not even cross our minds before: New York firefighters, that gay rugby player who helped bring down the fourth plane, bereaved families of so many national and ethnic origins. We even sometimes notice with a new attention the lives of Arab-Americans among us, or feel sympathy for a Sikh taxi driver who complains about customers who tell him to go home to "his country," even though he came to the United States as a political refugee from Punjab [India]. Sometimes our compassion even crosses that biggest line of all, the national boundary. Events have led many Americans to sympathize with the women and girls of Afghanistan, for example, in a way that many feminists had been trying to get people to do for a long time, without success.

Narrow Imaginations

All too often, however, our imaginations remain oriented to the local; indeed, this orientation is implicit in the unusual level of our alarm. The world has come to a stop in a way that it never has for Americans when disaster has befallen human beings in other places. Floods, earthquakes, cyclones—and the daily deaths of thousands from preventable malnutrition and disease—none of these typically make the American world come to a standstill, none elicit a tremendous outpouring of grief and compassion. The plight of innocent civilians in the current war evokes a similarly uneven and flickering response.

And worse: Our sense that the "us" is all that matters can easily flip over into a demonizing of an imagined "them," a group of outsiders who are imagined as enemies of the invulnerability and the pride of the all-important "us." Just as parents' compassion for their own children can all too easily slide into an attitude that promotes the defeat of other people's children, so too with patriotism: Compassion for our fellow Americans can all too easily slide over into an attitude that wants America to come out on top, defeating or subordinating other peoples or nations. Anger at the terrorists themselves is perfectly appropriate; so is the attempt to bring them to justice. But "us versus them" thinking doesn't always stay focused on the original issue; it too easily becomes a general call for American supremacy, the humiliation of "the other."

One vivid example of this slide took place at a baseball game I went to at Chicago's Comiskey Park, the first game played there after September 11—and a game against the Yankees, so there was a heightened awareness of the situation of New York and its people. Things began well, with a moving ceremony commemorating the firefighters who had lost their lives and honoring local firefighters who had gone to New York afterward to help out. There was even a lot of cheering when the Yankees took the field, a highly unusual transcendence of local attachments. But as the game went on and the beer flowed, one heard, increasingly, "U-S-A, U-S-A," echoing the chant from the 1980 Olympic hockey match in which the United States defeated Russia. This chant seemed to express a wish for America to defeat, abase, humiliate its enemies. Indeed, it soon became a general way of expressing the desire to crush one's enemies, whoever they were. When the umpire made a bad call that went against the Sox, the same group in the stands turned to him, chanting "U-S-A." In other words, anyone who crosses us is evil, and should be crushed. It's not surprising that Stoic philosopher and Roman emperor Marcus Aurelius, trying to educate himself to have an equal respect for all human beings, reported that his first lesson was "not to be a fan of the Greens or Blues at the races, or the light-armed or heavy-armed gladiators at the Circus."

The Nature of Compassion

Compassion is an emotion rooted, probably, in our biological heritage. (Although biologists once portrayed animal be-

True Patriotism

Today, we justly pledge allegiance to the republic for which America stands, but we do not have to pledge allegiance to the empire or failed policies for which America is now suffering. There are few finer, albeit painful, expressions of loyalty than to tell a friend, a spouse, a child, or a parent that what they are doing may be dangerous or wrong. If our country is about to run into the street without looking, there is absolutely nothing disloyal about crying, "Stop!"

True patriotism is an act of love, not of hate. It is debate not salutes, contributions not cheers, participation not prohibition, service not revenge. It's the product of vastly different people with remarkably similar dreams, for it is not a primeval past or cultural similarity that binds us but rather a shared present and future.

Sam Smith, *Yes! A Journal of Positive Futures*, Spring 2002.

---

havior as egoistic, primatologists by now recognize the existence of altruistic emotion in apes, and it may exist in other species as well.) But this history does not mean that compassion is devoid of thought. In fact, as Aristotle argued long ago, human compassion standardly requires three thoughts: that a serious bad thing has happened to someone else; that this bad event was not (or not entirely) the person's own fault; and that we ourselves are vulnerable in similar ways. Thus compassion forms a psychological link between our own self-interest and the reality of another person's good or ill. For that reason it is a morally valuable emotion—when it gets things right. Often, however, the thoughts involved in the emotion, and therefore the emotion itself, go astray, failing to link people at a distance to one's own current possibilities and vulnerabilities. (Rousseau said that kings don't feel compassion for their subjects because they count on never being human, subject to the vicissitudes of life.) Sometimes, too, compassion goes wrong by getting the seriousness of the bad event wrong: Sometimes, for example, we just don't take very seriously the hunger and illness of people who are distant from us. These errors are likely to be built into the nature of compassion as it develops in childhood and then adulthood: We form intense attachments to the local first, and only gradually learn to have compassion for people who are outside our own immediate circle. For many Americans, that expansion of moral concern stops at the national boundary.

Most of us are brought up to believe that all human beings have equal worth. At least the world's major religions and most secular philosophies tell us so. But our emotions don't believe it. We mourn for those we know, not for those we don't know. And most of us feel deep emotions about America, emotions we don't feel about India or Russia or Rwanda. In and of itself, this narrowness of our emotional lives is probably acceptable and maybe even good. We need to build outward from meanings we understand, or else our moral life would be empty of urgency. Aristotle long ago said, plausibly, that the citizens in Plato's ideal city, asked to care for all citizens equally, would actually care for none, since care is learned in small groups with their more intense attachments. Reading Marcus Aurelius bears this out: The project of weaning his imagination from its intense erotic attachments to the familial and the local gradually turns into the rather alarming project of weaning his heart from deep investment in the world. He finds that the only way to be utterly evenhanded is to cultivate a kind of death within life, seeing all people as distant and shadowlike, "vain images in a procession." If we want our life with others to contain strong passions—for justice in a world of injustice, for aid in a world where many go without what they need—we would do well to begin, at least, with our familiar strong emotions toward family, city and country. But concern should not stop with these local attachments.

Acknowledging Interdependence

Americans, unfortunately, are prone to such emotional narrowness. So are all people, but because of the power and geographical size of America, isolationism has particularly strong roots here. When at least some others were finding ways to rescue the Jews during the Holocaust, America's inactivity and general lack of concern were culpable, especially in proportion to American power. It took Pearl Harbor to get us even to come to the aid of our allies. When genocide was afoot in Rwanda, our own sense of self-sufficiency and invulnerability stopped us from imagining the Rwandans as people who might be us; we were therefore culpably inactive toward them. So too in the present situation. Sometimes we see a very laudable recognition of the interconnectedness of all peoples, and of the fact that we must join forces with people in all nations to defeat terrorists and bring them to justice. At other times, however, we see simplifying slogans ("America Fights Back") that portray the situation in terms of a good "us" crusading against an evil "them"—failing to acknowledge, for instance, that people in all nations have strong reasons to oppose terrorism, and that the fight has many active allies.

Such simplistic thinking is morally wrong, because it encourages us to ignore the impact of our actions on innocent civilians and to focus too little on the all-important project of humanitarian relief. It is also counterproductive. We now understand, or ought to, that if we had thought more about support for the educational and humanitarian infrastructure of Pakistan, for example, funding good local nongovernmental organizations there the way several European nations have done in India, young people in Pakistan might possibly have been educated in a climate of respect for religious pluralism, the equality of women and other values that we rightly prize instead of having fundamentalist madrassahs as their only educational option. Our policy in South Asia has exhibited for many years a gross failure of imagination and sympathy; we basically thought in terms of cold war values, ignoring the real lives of people to whose prospects our actions could make a great difference. Such crude thinking is morally obtuse; it is also badly calculated to advance any good cause we wish to embrace, in a world where all human lives are increasingly interdependent.

How to Extend Empathy

Compassion begins with the local. But if our moral natures and our emotional natures are to live in any sort of harmony, we must find devices through which to extend our strong emotions—and our ability to imagine the situation of others—to the world of human life as a whole. Since compassion contains thought, it can be educated. We can take this disaster as occasion for narrowing our focus, distrusting the rest of the world and feeling solidarity with Americans alone. Or we can take it as an occasion for expansion of our ethical horizons. Seeing how vulnerable our great country is, we can learn something about the vulnerability that all human beings share, about what it is like for distant others to lose those they love to a disaster not of their own making, whether it is hunger or flood or war.

Because human beings find the meaning of life in attachments that are local, we should not ask of people that they renounce patriotism, any more than we now ask them to renounce the love of their parents and children. But we typically do ask parents not to try to humiliate or thwart other people's children, and we work (at least sometimes) for schools that develop the abilities of all children, that try to make it possible for everyone to support themselves and find rewarding work. So too with the world: We may love our own nation most, but we should also strive for a world in which the capacities of human beings will not be blighted by hunger or misogyny or lack of education—or by being in the vicinity of a war one has not caused. We should therefore demand an education that does what it can to encourage the understanding of human predicaments—and also to teach children to recognize the many obstacles to that pursuit, the many pitfalls of the self-centered imagination as it tries to be just. There are hopeful signs in the present situation, particularly in attempts to educate the American public about Islam, about the histories of Afghanistan and Pakistan, and about the situation and attitudes of Arab-Americans in this country. But we need to make sure these educational efforts are consistent and systematic, not just fear-motivated responses to an immediate crisis.

Our media and our systems of education have long given us far too little information about lives outside our borders, stunting our moral imaginations. The situation of America's women and its racial, ethnic and sexual minorities has to some extent worked its way into curricula at various levels, and into our popular media. We have done less well with parts of the world that are unfamiliar. This is not surprising, because such teaching requires a lot of investment in new curricular initiatives, and such television programming requires a certain temporary inattention to the competition for ratings. But we now know that we live in a complex, inter-connected world, and we know our own ignorance. As Socrates said, this is at least the beginning of progress. At this time of national crisis we can renew our commitment to the equal worth of humanity, demanding media, and schools, that nourish and expand our imaginations by presenting non-American lives as deep, rich and compassion-worthy. "Thus from our weakness," said Rousseau of such an education, "our fragile happiness is born." Or, at least, it might be born.

"Multiculturalism . . . diminishes the sort of national identity and rightful patriotism that is the life's blood of the American order."

Valuing Diversity Is Not Patriotic

David Warren Saxe

Patriotism is a devotion to one's country that elicits a sense of duty and obedience to the national government, explains David Warren Saxe in the following viewpoint. American patriotism honors all who sacrificed their lives to defend the liberty, freedom, and justice that make the United States a great nation. Education that emphasizes diversity undermines U.S. patriotism because it promotes the idea that all cultures are equal and rejects the notion of American nationalism and supremacy, Saxe argues. If U.S. educators want to instill patriotism in their students, writes Saxe, they must reject multiculturalism and focus on teaching American history and heritage. Saxe teaches citizenship education at Pennsylvania State University in University Park. He is also the author of *Social Studies in Schools*.

As you read, consider the following questions:
1. According to Saxe, what is the basic obligation of public school teachers?
2. What does the word "patriotism" stem from, according to the author?
3. What are all factional interests subordinate to in America, according to Saxe?

David Warren Saxe, "Patriotism Versus Multiculturalism in Times of War," *Social Education*, vol. 67, March 2003, p. 107. Copyright © 2003 by National Council for the Social Studies. Reproduced by permission.

America is at war . . . again.[1] According to data supplied by the Naval Historical Center, from 1798 to 1993, America's forces have been used in 234 situations of conflict or potential conflict in the service of American interests. These 234 actions do not include our declared wars: War of 1812, Mexican War, Spanish-American War, World War I, and World War II. Nor do these actions include our undeclared wars against France, the Barbary Pirates, Korea, Vietnam, the Persian Gulf, and Iraq, or our recent engagements against [terrorist] Osama bin Laden as well as [Iraqi leader] Saddam Hussein. Finally, these 234 actions do not reflect routine stationing, training exercises, covert actions, or disaster relief.

Given these events together with all of the other military actions just described, one may argue that America has been in a perpetual state of "conflict" since our founding. The price of freedom is indeed "eternal vigilance."

While the nation is arguably under continuous threat, we need to ask: what is the responsibility of educators in a nation so engaged? Or, more plainly, what are the responsibilities of American educators in our republic?

Given our perennial obligation to defend the nation from all enemies—foreign and domestic—the task of educators in times of war is the same as that of educators in times of peace. Public school teachers have one basic obligation: in promoting the state, they must take up the mantle of embracing a love of nation—love of the land and our liberties—while they work to instill that same love within their students.

Love of Country

Love of nation begins early with a love for the land and love for the liberty that yields our rights. Young citizens should also learn to respect our national heroes, great and small, who sacrificed their treasure and often their lives so that we might enjoy our liberties. Love of nation also includes a respect and desire to learn more about its history, its great founding principles of life, liberty, and the pursuit of happiness, and our belief in equality and justice. Founding father

1. a reference to the U.S. war against Saddam Hussein's regime in Iraq in 2003

John Wilson of Pennsylvania put it best: "Law and liberty cannot rationally become the objects of our love, unless they first become the objects of our knowledge." To fulfill this hope, teachers are needed to supply the necessary knowledge found in careful study and teaching of American history and civics.

As our military prepares in times of peace for war, our schools must do the same. And what is the proper education in times of peace and war? In a word, patriotism. Patriotism in schools is what preparedness is to the military. It is a promissory note of citizenship, a gift to the nation, and an insurance policy for liberty and our American way of life. In our republic, just as a prepared military is necessary, a prepared and informed civilian population is not only necessary but is also vital to national survival. And what is this patriotism that prepares citizens for peace and war with equal attention?

At its root, patriotism is the love and devotion to one's country that prompts a meaningful obedience and loyalty to its government. Patriotism isn't just participating in local, state, and federal governments; it is recognizing the duty we hold not just for ourselves and families but also for all members of our society. Our duty to serve the whole community—to consider the needs of every citizen in the serious promotion of the general welfare—defines the sort of patriotism that should be sponsored in schools.

The word patriotism stems from a Greek term meaning "the notion of coming from our forefathers." Applied to schools, patriotism is an acknowledgement to those who came before us, those who founded our great nation and its splendid laws and institutions, an acknowledgement to those who sacrificed for us, those who died fighting for our freedoms, maintaining our liberties, seeking and securing justice, an acknowledgement and recognition to those who serviced the nation's needs, answering the nation's call, defending our fights, citizens, borders, and interests.

Patriotism is a solemn recognition of gratitude for those who came before us, those who gave something and sometimes all of themselves, those who sacrificed for benefits realized only by the modern holders of the title "citizen." In sum, patriotism is about the love of country and the respectful remembrance of those who gave that love for our benefit. We have this great nation because those patriots in the past loved their country and loved it enough to sacrifice and die for it.

Diversity Versus Patriotism

In the past two decades, an educational program has come into the schools displacing what used to serve as history and civics education, effectively rejecting the early dictum of one nation, one people. This new social studies program, known as multiculturalism or diversity, features the study of many cultures and even subcultures under the dictum that all cultures are equal, are worthy, and should be respected, and finally, in keeping with this logic, no one culture is superior to any other. In this model of America, there is no common culture, no common heritage, no core principles, and no single nation of one sovereign people.

As this revolution challenged the once unquestioned E Pluribus Unum in the schools, it also transformed National Council for the Social Studies [NCSS]. With a long-term focus on global issues, the so-called inclusive curriculum fit nicely with the demands and expectations of NCSS policies and programs. However, the older focus on American citizenship based on solid American history (long absent from NCSS programs and policies) became a casualty as NCSS remade itself into the premier institution for multicultural and diversity curricula. On this point, NCSS should be congratulated for its singular devotion and consistency in promoting the special interest agenda encased in multicultural theory and practice.

Despite the success of the suddenly inclusive curricula in schools, social studies as multiculturalism as a masthead of citizenship education is not a particularly effective or inviting method to promote American nationalism. If social studies–multiculturalism sought only to promote a respectful international cooperation within the policies and laws of the United States, where Americans are cautioned to pause and consider the "other" in light of American interests, all is well. But if the policies and laws of the United States differ with other nations or the United Nations (a favored institution of multiculturalists) or with the dictates of social studies–multiculturalism, public schools must defer to the original configuration of public schools as public instruments and agencies of the United States of America.

We are not "all multiculturalists" as Nathan Glazer once gushed. American public school teachers are, first of all, paid employees of the state, and those teachers charged with citizenship education are agents of our founding principles responsible for the civic education of all students. Public school teachers are not workers for the United Nations nor are they agents of the special interest group, National Council for the Social Studies. The disconnect between special interest associations and the proper role of state employees cannot be overstated: the loyalty and duty of American teachers is clear—American interests as defined through our legitimate legislative process in concert with our laws seated in the U.S. Constitution supersede the special interests of any other entity, foreign or domestic.

What Citizenship Education Requires

The idea that the interests of the United States as a sovereign nation are superior to all other concerns is not clearly understood by educators who have not or will not accept that the primacy of citizenship education centered on American sovereignty runs counter to the internationalist, social studies–multicultural dogma. Sadly, uninformed and misinformed practitioners often make no distinctions between special interest groups such as NCSS and the U.S. government. This should not be the case. Quite plainly, a state curriculum that posits international human rights doctrines and seeks to foster and promote a global identity as superior to our constitutional obligations is patently wrong for American public schools. Our Founding Fathers invented a system of government devoted to equality, justice, and peace, which, in its explicit theory (as revealed in the Federalist Papers), is fully cognizant of the realities of human nature, recognizing the failures of men and of their governments. These recognitions were derived from a careful study of history and the actions of mankind. This study of history and the actions of mankind is the same one that all teachers engaged in citizenship education should encourage with their students. From such studies, the founders presented the marvelous vision of a great American nation constructed with "auxiliary precautions" to mitigate against the darker forces of humanity and carefully designed to hold in check those who would usurp the legitimate power and rights of citizens for personal interests.

In brief, in the ancient business of war and of government, the social justice theory underlining social studies–multiculturalism evaporates in the true light of human events, in the due course of human nature, and in the light of American national interests. When pressed in our schools, social studies–multiculturalism is at best nothing more than indoctrination of foolish notions. At its worst, it has come to be the obnoxious application of factional interests run amok. As taught, social studies–multiculturalism highlights the divisive nature of ethnicity and other group characteristics and imprudently diminishes the sort of national identity and rightful patriotism that is the life's blood of the American order. In sum, social studies–multiculturalism is not consistent with nationalism and American sovereignty in any form, nor is social studies–multiculturalism compatible with a patriotism that seeks to endear citizens to this nation, the American nation with its Union, its constitutional framework of laws, and its republican form of government.

Multiculturalist Poison

Patriotism is dying a slow death, poisoned by revisionists, multiculturalists, advocates of hyphenated identity and an elite that disparages our history and heritage and rejects our ideals (a worldview that used to be called "the American way").

Thanks to their ceaseless efforts, young Americans no longer learn their history, celebrate their heroes or grasp their nation's uniqueness.

Don Feder, *Insight on the News*, June 4, 2001.

What renders social studies–multiculturalism invalid for national educational policy is that it highlights the many at the expense of the one. In turning E Pluribus Unum on its head, social studies–multiculturalism pits citizen against citizen by the most base of characteristics: race, gender, ethnicity, sexual orientation, and other such divisions. A citizenship education centered on the sort of patriotism that promotes a national character, a unity amid diverse factional interests, and a conception of one nation, one people holds no place for hyphenated-citizens. In contrast, a social studies–multiculturalism that recognizes no national sovereignty, celebrates no common culture, and triumphs the hyphenated American is patently a contradiction in terms and engenders a confliction of loyalties. Here, in this salad bowl of cultures, government is transformed into a game of special interests seeking and expecting special attention from the many for the benefit of the few.

Factional Interests

Is there no place for factional interests such as National Council for the Social Studies in public schools under its present multicultural banner? Must all be for the one, for the nation? The founders provided an answer; they invented a government in full recognition of the natural state of human affairs to split into factional interests. Where history proved that factional interests were almost always at the root of domestic upheaval, often providing opportunities for rival powers to capitalize on the weakness of division, the founders welcomed factional interests. However, all factional interests must still operate under the banner of the United States of America.

In the founding of the United States, the authors of our Constitution embraced factional interests as a strength, not a weakness. In their remarkable and time-tested theory, as detailed in the magnificent Federalist Papers, the founders envisioned a continental power of many people with many diverse interests (see especially Federalist 10 and 51).

The authority for public schools to teach a reasoned patriotism rests in the Constitution's guarantee clause as found in Article IV, Section 4. "The United States shall guarantee to every State in this Union a Republican Form of Government." What better way to ensure the Union than for its public school teachers to promote an educated and reasoned, yet still undivided patriotism with our young citizens.

As a factional interest group, NCSS is entitled to promote the policies and programs of its members within the context of NCSS membership. However, NCSS has no more authority to direct the educational programs of American public schools than has the Catholic Church or Democratic Party. In sum, public schools belong to the public, the whole public, and as such, are not the exclusive domain of factional interest groups such as NCSS, with its global-multicultural-diversity curricula. Any illegitimate intrusion of factional interests into the policies and practices of American public schools must be considered at best inappropriate and at worst inexcusable, and where found in abuse, citizens have an obligation to dismantle and erase its programs.

Whatever passes as American citizenship education should instill patriotism as job one, and such instruction should be the same in peace as in war. The curriculum of social studies–multiculturalism, social justice theory, and/or diversity studies is nothing more than factional interests that should and must be checked by the cool reason of constitutional restrictions and guarantees. Factional interests as national public school policies and practices are antithetical to patriotism and American nationalism, wholly incompatible with our Constitution, and undermine the prospects of our national survival.

A Debt of Gratitude

The United States is a great nation. In times of war and in times of peace, we should recognize the founders and those who stood on their shoulders to build this nation. We owe a debt of gratitude to the patriots of our past, and we have an obligation to ourselves and our posterity to effect the best means for our national survival together as one people.

The course is clear. Any individual employed by the state to teach the greatest asset of this nation's future, our youth, is obligated to deliver on the guarantee clause of the U.S. Constitution as found in Article IV, Section, 4. There is no better way to ensure "our republican form of government" than to instill in the next generation of citizens a love of our land and our liberty. The best proven means of instilling this love is through a devoted study of the fundamentals of

American history and the principles of American government aligned to the imperative of one nation, one people.

There is no question that the words "American history" and "civics" are found in the conversation of NCSS apologists. However, it is not the mouthing of words that is at issue; it is action predicated on our civic duty as American educators, not agents for special interest groups. Unhappily, National Council for the Social Studies, as found in its policies and standards, abandoned such dedicated teaching long ago.

"*Rather than blind conformity to the current regime, patriotism could just as easily mean openly embracing the progressive ideals upon which the nation was founded.*"

Patriotism and Liberalism Are Compatible

Craig Cox

American progressives often perceive contemporary patriotism as political conformity, support for war, and nationalistic arrogance, writes Craig Cox in the following viewpoint. Furthermore, he points out, when liberals disagree with government policy, conservatives often accuse them of being unpatriotic or traitorous. However, progressive ideals—such as a commitment to social justice, equal opportunity, civil liberties, and the right to dissent—are significant contributions to the American experiment. Patriotism can be celebrated as an expression of these important liberal values, Cox maintains. Cox is the executive editor of the *Utne Reader*, a bimonthly progressive journal.

As you read, consider the following questions:
1. According to the author, what did Francis Bellamy, the author of the Pledge of Allegiance, hope to promote?
2. What famous American idealists is Cox proud to wave the flag for?
3. What patriotic efforts could progressives pursue, in Cox's opinion?

During the 1991 war with Iraq, my father-in-law gave me a flag. It came with an easily assembled pole and bracket designed to display Old Glory at a 45-degree angle on the front porch of our bungalow. I thanked him and stuffed it into the bedroom closet after he left.

On subsequent visits, he never asked me about the flag. I thought at the time that he, a Navy veteran of World War II and a staunch Republican, was just goading his goofy leftist son-in-law and former Air Force sergeant—daring me to shed my dissident pretenses and get with the program. I never did, but I sometimes catch myself wondering what I—and other progressive-minded folks—give up by refusing to play the patriot game.

Politically, the price is pretty obvious: Conservatives tar and feather us as enemies of the state and dismiss our opinions as the poisonous rants of traitors. Meanwhile, the president pops in at a flag factory for a photo op and his approval ratings jump a half dozen points.

Progressive Patriotism

We all know that patriotism runs a lot deeper than flying the flag on the Fourth of July or mumbling our way through the "Star Spangled Banner" at a football game. It is more often defined these days by blind political conformity, an almost pathological readiness to make war, and a shocking betrayal of civil liberties. But what alternative do progressives offer? How do we seize the patriotic high ground?

The easy answer, of course, is to lighten up, embrace the symbols of national pride with the same shallowness as our political leaders, and get back to the real work of social change. Maybe we'll fool enough people enough of the time to regain our political footing and make a point or two about the minor flaws of our otherwise fabulously great nation. Failing that, we might want to drill down to that core of patriotic ambivalence inside each of us and identify the things we really *do* love about this country and find ways to celebrate them.

To hear longtime left activists Peter Dreier and Dick Flacks tell it, we might start by remembering our history. Writing in *The Nation* (June 3, 2002), Dreier and Flacks remind us that many of our nation's most treasured patriotic symbols were created and promoted by left-leaning Americans hungry for social change.

Take those inspiring lines inscribed on the Statue of Liberty, "Give me your tired, your poor / Your huddled masses yearning to breathe free." They were penned by poet Emma Lazarus, a supporter of Henry George's "socialistic" single-tax program. Or check out the origins of "America the Beautiful." The lyrics were written in 1893 by poet Katharine Lee Bates, an anti-imperialist university professor active in Boston progressive reform movements. Even that perennial political football the Pledge of Allegiance has progressive roots. It was authored in 1892 by Francis Bellamy, a prominent Christian socialist at the time who, according to Dreier and Flacks, hoped that the pledge would "promote a moral vision to counter the individualism embodied in capitalism and expressed in the climate of the Gilded Age." (Remember, "under God" was added by Congress in 1954 during the Red Scare.)

More recently, Aaron Copland created his symphonic classics *Fanfare for the Common Man* and *Lincoln Portrait*, two Independence Day favorites, in the 1930s, when he was part of a composers collective dedicated to writing music that honored the working class. And America's unofficial national anthem. "This Land Is Your Land," was written in 1940, when folk singer/songwriter Woody Guthrie was well connected with the Communist Party.

"The progressive authors of much of America's patriotic iconography rejected blind nationalism, militaristic drumbeating, and sheeplike conformism," write Dreier and Flacks. "So it would be a dire mistake to allow, by default, jingoism to become synonymous with patriotism and the American spirit."

A Different World

Twenty-first-century America, of course, is a different world from the country that spawned these progressives of the Gilded Age and the Great Depression. Theirs was largely an immigrant culture whose memory of injustices on foreign shores served as a daily reminder of America's promise. And there was, I think, a sense of wonder that still surrounded the American experiment, a feeling perhaps that our democratic structures and civic commons were still capable of being shaped by regular people. It was, in other words, a flag worth waving.

Immigrants still stream to our borders with hopes of a better life, but today it's hard to think of the USA as a work in progress. Its political culture is rigid and systemized. Its economy rules the world; its military might is virtually unchallenged. Its astounding affluence argues more eloquently against dissent than any patriotic rhetoric. It is, in many ways, the country many of our forebears dreamed it would be.

Still, it's hard to sing the praises of a nation whose leaders regularly treat the rest of the world with open contempt and whose dominant culture glorifies getting over giving. From the point of view of other countries in the global community, you have to admit, America is not always a good neighbor. We play our music too loud, drive our vehicles all over

Wheeler. © 2002 by Shannon Wheeler. Reproduced by permission of *Utne Reader* and Shannon Wheeler.

everyone else's lawns, and like to shoot out the streetlights on the weekends.

Yes, we are richly blessed. And, yes, I'd rather be living here than trapped in the terrifying squalor of a Palestinian refugee camp or in a cinder-block apartment building amid the political and economic chaos of post-communist Russia. But that doesn't mean I need to run Old Glory up the flag-pole every time American soldiers are deployed somewhere around the world or my local Chevy dealer announces a factory clearance sale.

A Flag Worth Waving

But what does it mean to be progressively patriotic? How do we celebrate a love of country in a way that feels authentic, in a way that honors the strides we've made and recognizes those we still need to make? Remembering our history is a good start—acknowledging the power the American idea held for those who came before us, and working to keep it alive for those who will follow. I can proudly wave the flag in memory of Dr. Martin Luther King Jr. and Rosa Parks, Margaret Sanger and Susan B. Anthony, Samuel Gompers and Cesar Chavez.

I can also be an unabashed patriot for my neighborhood and happily pledge my allegiance to folks down the street who pitch in when one of us is in need. And I'll wave the flag gladly to celebrate our all-American right to be left alone by government, and for our free press, and for the privilege of challenging our elected representatives.

I'd also argue that patriotism does not need to focus only on national holidays. I rather like thinking of our annual May Day Festival in south Minneapolis as a patriotic occasion. Here we are, 10 or 20 thousand souls basking in the first marvelous days of spring and espousing all sorts of lefty, anarcho-pagan beliefs, and I'd like somebody, just once, to unfurl an American flag and stubbornly hold court about how it's a pretty great country that doesn't send out the National Guard to shut this thing down.

Why not unfurl the flag next time you march against some local injustice, reveling in the rights our nation bestows on dissenters? Why not belt out "America the Beautiful" next time you picket in support of an environmental or labor cause? It might remind you and your comrades of the shoulders you're standing on.

Rather than blind conformity to the current regime, patriotism could just as easily mean openly embracing the progressive ideals upon which the nation was founded—corny old 18th-century concepts like liberty, equality, justice, and freedom—and attaching them to the issues we care about. Fair wages for service employees, equal opportunity for immigrants, and affordable housing for the homeless can all be seen as patriotic efforts.

A Powerful Message

No matter where we focus our patriotic efforts, we first need to shed the conceit that tells us that any identification with the flag is just frivolous symbolism that links us with [President] George W. Bush, [Attorney General] John Ashcroft, [Vice President] Dick Cheney, and [Secretary of Defense] Donald Rumsfeld. That is not true.

As we saw so vividly in the aftermath of 9/11, patriotism is a powerful message that touches millions of ordinary Americans, many of whom disagree with the current administration on important issues and would welcome a progressive political alternative. By disavowing or ridiculing these symbols, we lose an opportunity to reach those people with ideas they may also embrace.

But this is not just about forwarding a set of political ideas or winning elections. It's about reclaiming a share of a cultural tradition that binds us together as a people. It's about *participating* again in the big conversation that is supposed to be the American experiment.

So I'm going to take that flag out of my closet and fly it proudly, for my own reasons. Let's stand up for our country—at least those progressive values deep at the heart of the American idea. Go ahead: qualify, equivocate, blush even. I know I will. But let's find our own unique patriotism and blast our message with all its ambivalence to the rest of the world. It won't stop politicians from wrapping themselves in the flag, but it just might keep them from using it to smother the rest of us.

"A person who regularly denounces America as bigoted, corrupt, and a cancer on the planet . . . might be marginally less patriotic than your average volunteer firefighter."

The Patriotism of Some Liberals Is Questionable

Jonah Goldberg

In the following viewpoint Jonah Goldberg contends that it has become politically incorrect to question anyone's patriotism. Liberal pundits, in particular, often charge that those who question their patriotism are engaging in the kind of political loyalty tests that became infamous during the Cold War era. However, Goldberg states, some left-wingers claim that America is an oppressive, greedy, and exploitative nation, and they challenge the supremacy of American institutions. It is not immoral or unfair to suggest that these liberals are unpatriotic, the author concludes. Goldberg is a syndicated columnist and the editor of *National Review Online*, a conservative journal of opinion.

As you read, consider the following questions:

1. According to Goldberg, how does American patriotism differ from Spartan patriotism?
2. In the author's opinion, why does the left want to make patriotism politically irrelevant?
3. In what way have liberals questioned the compassion of conservatives, according to Goldberg?

"**I**t is . . . clear how wrong the president was to sit back and let his political pals orchestrate a campaign to question the patriotism of those who urged a full national debate" on war with Iraq, writes Tom Oliphant of the *Boston Globe*. *New York Times* columnist Paul Krugman concurs, "The Bush administration," he writes, is "always quick to question the patriotism of anyone who gets in its way." And the *Economist* has observed: "Republican candidates for this autumn's [2002] elections speak with a single voice. Defend the tax cut; pump up spending on the war on terror; praise the president; and—sotto voce—question the patriotism of anyone who criticises him."

But is all of this true? Is the White House really casting doubt on its critics' love of country? Maybe a little, though Krugman & Co. rarely provide evidence to back up such accusations. But the facts are beside the point, because the question of patriotism, or the lack of it, constitutes the oldest form of political correctness in America. All you need to do is question whether someone is questioning your patriotism and you've already won the argument. It's very similar to the accusation of "going negative" in political campaigns: The charge that your opponent is unfairly attacking you is in itself a form of attack against which, apparently, there is no defense. Similarly, it seems the only response to the charge that you've impugned someone's love of country is to back down completely. "No, no, I would never question anyone's patriotism" is the standard capitulation.

The Distaste for Wedge-Issue Patriotism

There are a number of reasons for this healthy distaste for making patriotism a wedge issue. First, as Walter Berns noted in his book *Making Patriots*, America is a nation founded upon individual rights. American patriotism, therefore, is the opposite of Spartan patriotism, which was a love of the State above all else. Patriotism in America is rightly defined as a love for the institutions that keep us free. Since American patriotism is less about blood and soil than it is about ideas, patriots must recognize that political dissent is politically loyal.

Another, less salubrious historical source of this distaste is the terrible spectacle of the McCarthy period [during the Cold War]. Joe McCarthy challenged the loyalty of many Americans, which is, to be sure, an ugly thing to do. He was certainly right about the disloyalty of some Americans; still, the Left has won the propaganda war over that period and now calls into question the idea that anybody can ever be accused of a lack of patriotism. Sure, Ethel and Julius Rosenberg can be executed for treason; but never, ever doubt their love of America![1]

And so now, a point of political good manners has evolved into a cliché disguised as a moral fact: It is never right to question anyone's patriotism. And this is absurd. Surely Robert Hanssen, Aldrich Ames, and Jonathan Pollard were less patriotic than, say, Sgt. York?[2] There must be rational ways to deduce that someone is relatively more patriotic than someone else. A person who regularly denounces America as bigoted, corrupt, and a cancer on the planet, one might reasonably assume, might be marginally less patriotic than your average volunteer firefighter or VFW hall manager.

The Iraqi News Agency recently reported, for example, that [U.S. Nation of Islam leader] Louis Farrakhan told the Iraqi Islamic Affairs minister [during the U.S. war against Iraq in 2003] that "the Muslim American people are praying to the almighty God to grant victory to Iraq." He claims to have been misquoted, but whether he said it or not, it is reasonable to say that Farrakhan's actions are not brimming with patriotism, especially when taken in the context of his other comments about the United States.

When Is Patriotism Relevant?

So what? Does it matter if someone isn't patriotic? Of course it does, in some contexts. Irreligious hot-dog vendors aren't a big deal; irreligious priests and rabbis, on the other hand, can be a serious problem for their respective religions. Similarly, an unpatriotic plumber isn't much of a threat to the Republic; an unpatriotic politician just might be. Take an

1. Ethel and Julius Rosenberg were executed for the crime of espionage in 1953.
2. Hanssen, Ames, and Pollard were all convicted of espionage. Sergeant Alvin York was a World War I hero.

obvious example: As pressure builds for the U.S. to surrender its sovereignty to various international bodies, it seems perfectly relevant to inquire into a politician's commitment to the supremacy of American institutions. If you are of the Noam Chomsky school and believe that the story of America is a story of exploitation, greed, and oppression, it follows that you will be sympathetic to the arguments of foreign critics and much more open to the "ameliorative" laws, regulations, and treaties offered by the United Nations and the like. If you believe that America was put on this earth to launch some full-tilt boogie for freedom and justice, however, then you will likely be more skeptical of innovations like the International Criminal Court.

The America-Hating Left

Most of the America-despising left has fallen silent since [the terrorist attacks of] September 11 [2001]. But not all. Katha Pollitt, in the *Nation* magazine, writes: "My daughter, who goes to Stuveysant High School only blocks from the World Trade Center, thinks we should fly an American flag out our window. Definitely not, I say: The flag stands for jingoism and vengeance and war. . . ."

In the *New Yorker*, [writer] Susan Sontag condemns "the unanimity of the sanctimonious, reality-concealing rhetoric spouted by American officials and media commentators." Like Pollitt, Sontag will fly no flag from her living room. "'Our country is strong,' we are told again and again," she writes. "I for one don't find this entirely consoling."

It would be a mistake to think that these writers are cranks. The anti-American impulse of the left has been a constant feature of our national life for at least 70 years.

Mona Charen, *Conservative Chronicle*, October 10, 2001.

To those of an "international" outlook, patriotism is an atavistic passion—in Bertrand Russell's words, "the willingness to kill and be killed for trivial reasons." It's entirely understandable, therefore, that the broadly defined Left, as the self-anointed fixer of history, would want to de-legitimize patriotism as a political issue. And the best way to do this is to respond to questions about your patriotism by leveling accusations of McCarthyism at your critic. During one of the

1992 presidential debates, President [George H.W.] Bush commented, "I think it's wrong to demonstrate against your own country or organize demonstrations against your own country on foreign soil." Gov. [Bill] Clinton shot back: "Your father was right to stand up to Joe McCarthy. You were wrong to attack my patriotism. I was opposed to the war, but I love my country." Okay, but Prescott Bush's disagreements with Sen. McCarthy notwithstanding, does that mean Clinton's anti-American protests on foreign soil weren't a legitimate issue? Given Clinton's record of apologizing for America's sins around the world and his eagerness to sign up for various U.N. schemes, it seems that maybe his youthful indiscretions weren't entirely irrelevant to his presidency.

Unfortunately, the Left's strategy has worked. Indeed, pretty much any argument that makes liberals look bad is now called McCarthyism of some kind. Even though the vast majority of liberal politicians could defuse patriotism as an issue with a few words—as evidenced by their mad dash to denounce the recent Pledge decision[3]—it still makes them uncomfortable enough to accuse conservatives of fascism when they bring it up.

A Politically Correct Fiction

But if conservatives content themselves with appeasing the delicate sensibilities of liberals, then conservatism will become meaningless. It would be better if conservatives stopped paying tribute to the politically correct fiction that patriotism is an unquantifiable and irrelevant barbarism, and took the issue head-on instead of speaking in code. It's no wonder so many liberals imagine conservatives question their love of America, when so many conservatives wink when they say they don't.

One thing we should ask those on the left who claim patriotism is an illegitimate issue is: Why is it so much worse to question someone's patriotism than to question his humanity? Conservatives have their compassion—for the young, the old, and the poor—questioned almost hourly. [Senators]

3. a reference to a June 2002 federal appeals court ruling that reciting the Pledge of Allegiance in public schools is an unconstitutional endorsement of religion

Dick Gephardt and Tom Daschle frame almost every issue in terms of Democrats who "care" about blacks, gays, the old, the young, the sick, the poor, the handicapped, etc., versus Republicans who "don't care about" (that is to say, who hate) these same categories of people.

Bill Clinton regularly demanded that Congress pass legislation that, in his words, "lifts people up without punishing children"—the assumption being that those who disagreed with his approach might be willing to punish children. The Million Mom March was in a sense couched in maternal McCarthyism: You're not a "real" mother if you don't support gun control. Jesse Jackson suggests, all the time, that conservatives are Nazis. While serving as Al Gore's campaign manager, Donna Brazile infamously declared that Republicans "have no love and no joy. They'd rather take pictures with black children than feed them."

Indeed, Al Gore's "people versus the powerful" campaign flatly asserted that Gore cared more about Americans than Bush did. But for some reason, the question of who cares more about Americans is the essence of responsible politics, but the question of who cares more about America is a gross perversion of what it means to be an American. Surely, if it's fair to suggest that conservatives are racists, warmongers, child-haters, Dickensian ogres, and unfit mothers, there's a smidgen of room to suggest that some liberals don't like America as much as we do.

*"[War] does not enable the pursuit of
happiness but brings despair and grief."*

Supporting War Is Not Patriotic

Howard Zinn

In the viewpoint that follows, Howard Zinn expresses his disagreement with the U.S. government's decision to go to war against Iraq in 2003. Americans who die in this conflict, he argues, will not have died for their country but for a government motivated by greed and power. True American patriots are inspired by their country's dedication to democracy and human rights, not by their government's push for global dominance. War contradicts America's promise to promote liberty and protect human life; thus, war should not receive the support of U.S. patriots. Zinn, the author of *A People's History of the United States*, is a columnist for the *Progressive*.

As you read, consider the following questions:

1. According to the Declaration of Independence, when should Americans alter or abolish their government?
2. According to Mark Twain, quoted by Zinn, what is "monarchical patriotism"?
3. How should patriotism be redefined, in Zinn's view?

Howard Zinn, "Dying for the Government," *The Progressive*, vol. 67, June 2003, p. 16. Copyright © 2003 by The Progressive, Inc., 409 E. Main St., Madison, WI 53703. www.progressive.org. Reproduced by permission.

Our government has declared a military victory in Iraq [in 2003]. As a patriot, I will not celebrate. I will mourn the dead—the American GIs, and also the Iraqi dead, of whom there have been many, many more.

I will mourn the Iraqi children, not just those who are dead, but those who have been blinded, crippled, disfigured, or traumatized. We have not been given in the American media (we would need to read the foreign press) a full picture of the human suffering caused by our bombing.

We got precise figures for the American dead, but not for the Iraqis. Recall [Secretary of State] Colin Powell after the first Gulf War, when he reported the "small" number of U.S. dead, and when asked about the Iraqi dead, replied: "That is really not a matter I am terribly interested in."

As a patriot, contemplating the dead GIs, I could comfort myself (as, understandably, their families do) with the thought: "They died for their country." But I would be lying to myself.

Dying for the Government

Those who died in this war did not die for their country. They died for their government. They died for Bush and Cheney and Rumsfeld.[1] And yes, they died for the greed of the oil cartels, for the expansion of the American empire, for the political ambitions of the President. They died to cover up the theft of the nation's wealth to pay for the machines of death.

The distinction between dying for your country and dying for your government is crucial in understanding what I believe to be the definition of patriotism in a democracy. According to the Declaration of Independence—the fundamental document of democracy—governments are artificial creations, established by the people, "deriving their just powers from the consent of the governed," and charged by the people to ensure the equal right of all to "life, liberty, and the pursuit of happiness." Furthermore, as the Declaration says, "whenever any form of government becomes destructive of these ends, it is the right of the people to alter or abolish it."

It is the country that is primary—the people, the ideals of

1. President George W. Bush, Vice President Dick Cheney, and Secretary of Defense Donald Rumsfeld

the sanctity of human life and the promotion of liberty. When a government recklessly expends the lives of its young for crass motives of profit and power, always claiming that its motives are pure and moral ("Operation Just Cause" was the invasion of Panama and "Operation Iraqi Freedom" in the present instance), it is violating its promise to the country. War is almost always a breaking of that promise. It does not enable the pursuit of happiness but brings despair and grief.

Monarchical Patriotism

Mark Twain, having been called a "traitor" for criticizing the U.S. invasion of the Philippines, derided what he called "monarchical patriotism." He said: "The gospel of the monarchical patriotism is: 'The King can do no wrong.' we have adopted it with all its servility, with an unimportant change in the wording: 'Our country, right or wrong!' We have thrown away the most valuable asset we had—the individual's right to oppose both flag and country when he believed them to be in the wrong. We have thrown it away; and with it, all that was really respectable about that grotesque and laughable word, Patriotism."

If patriotism in the best sense (not in the monarchical sense) is loyalty to the principles of democracy, then who was the true patriot. Theodore Roosevelt, who applauded a massacre by American soldiers of 600 Filipino men, women, and children on a remote Philippine island, or Mark Twain, who denounced it?

With the war in Iraq won, shall we revel in American military power and—against the history of modern empires—insist that the American empire will be beneficent?

Our own history, shows something different. It begins with what was called, in our high school history classes, "westward expansion"—a euphemism for the annihilation or expulsion of the Indian tribes inhabiting the continent, all in the name of "progress" and "civilization." It continues with the expansion of American power into the Caribbean at the turn of the [twentieth] century, then into the Philippines, and then repeated Marine invasions of Central America and long military occupations of Haiti and the Dominican Republic.

After World War II, Henry Luce, owner of *Time, Life,* and *Fortune,* spoke of "the American Century," in which this country would organize the world "as we see fit." Indeed, the expansion of American power continued, too often supporting military dictatorships in Asia, Africa, Latin America, the Middle East, because they were friendly to American corporations and the American government.

The record does not justify confidence in Bush's boast that the United States will bring democracy to Iraq. Should Americans welcome the expansion of the nation's power, with the anger this has generated among so many people in the world? Should we welcome the huge growth of the military budget at the expense of health, education, the needs of children, one fifth of whom grow up in poverty?

I suggest that a patriotic American who cares for his or her country might act on behalf of a different vision. Instead of being feared for our military prowess, we should want to be respected for our dedication to human rights.

Should we not begin to redefine patriotism? We need to expand it beyond that narrow nationalism that has caused so much death and suffering. If national boundaries should not be obstacles to trade—some call it "globalization"—should they also not be obstacles to compassion and generosity?

Should we not begin to consider all children, everywhere, as our own? In that case, war, which in our time is always an assault on children, would be unacceptable as a solution to the problems of the world. Human ingenuity would have to search for other ways.

*"The 'Peace' Movement isn't about peace.
. . . It's about carrying on the left's war
against America."*

Supporting the Peace Movement Is Not Patriotic

David Horowitz

Columnist David Horowitz is a cofounder of the Center for the Study of Popular Culture, an educational organization that monitors political correctness and multiculturalism in the media and in academia. In the following viewpoint Horowitz contends that today's so-called peace movement is really a cabal of anti-American radicals who blame the world's sufferings on the United States. If left to their own devices, Horowitz claims, this movement will create divisiveness among Americans and make it more difficult for the U.S. government to secure real peace.

As you read, consider the following questions:
1. According to Horowitz, what groups have anti-American radicals supported in the past?
2. In the mind of the peace radical, who is to blame for the 2001 terrorist attacks on the United States, according to Horowitz?
3. What happened after America was forced to abandon Indochina during the Cold War, according to the author?

David Horowitz, "The Peace Movement Isn't About Peace," www.FrontPage Magazine.com, January 21, 2003. Copyright © 2003 by FrontPageMagazine.com. Reproduced by permission.

The "Peace" Movement isn't about peace. . . . It's about carrying on the left's war against America. When your country is attacked, when the enemy has targeted every American regardless of race, gender or age for death, there can be no "peace" movement. There can only be a movement that divides Americans and gives aid and comfort to our enemies.

In his speech to Congress after [the terrorist attacks of September 11, 2001] the President said: "We have seen their kind before. They are the heirs of all the murderous ideologies of the 20th Century. By sacrificing human life to serve their radical visions, by abandoning every value except the will to power, they follow in the path of fascism, Nazism and totalitarianism."

The so-called "peace movement" today is led by the same hate-America radicals who supported America's totalitarian enemies during the Cold War. They marched in support of the Vietcong, the Sandinista Marxists and the Communist guerrillas in El Salvador. Before that they marched in behalf of [Communist leaders] Stalin and Mao. They still support [Cuban leader Fidel] Castro and the nuclear lunatic in North Korea, Kim Jong-Il. They are the friends in deed of [terrorist mastermind] Osama bin Laden and [then Iraqi leader] Saddam Hussein.

What prompts American radicals to make common cause with such monsters? The answer is obvious: They share a common view of America as the "Great Satan." They believe that it is America—not tyrants like Saddam Hussein—that inflicts misery and suffering on the world. The targets of the 9/11 terrorists were Wall Street and the Pentagon. These were the targets of American radicals long before.

In the perverse minds of the so-called "peace" radicals, America is the "root cause" of all the root causes that inspire the terrorists to attack us. "America is to blame for what is wrong in the world. The enemy is us."

Dividing the Home Front

Today, as we battle the Axis of Evil[1] which threatens us with weapons of mass destruction, these familiar mantras are ris-

1. Iran, Iraq, and North Korea—considered to be hostile regimes because they are attempting to develop weapons of mass destruction

ing on college campuses from coast to coast. Just as they did in the Cold War past.

During the Cold War, the radical "peace" movement bullied right-thinking Americans into silence. Our government lost the ability to stay the course in the anti-Communist war. The result was the Communist slaughter of two-and-a-half million peasants in Indo-China after the divisions at home forced America to leave.

Heller. © 2003 by Joe Heller. Reproduced by permission.

Once again, the hate America left is attempting to silence right-thinking citizens. It is attempting to divide the home front in the face of the enemy. Even as we go to war. It is stabbing our young men and women in the back even as they step into harm's way to defend us. It is attempting to paralyze our government again and prevent it from securing the peace.

We can't afford to let this happen. The time has come for those who love freedom and who appreciate the great bounties of this nation to stand up and be counted.

Periodical Bibliography

The following articles have been selected to supplement the diverse views presented in this chapter.

Max Boot	"The Case for American Empire," *Weekly Standard*, October 15, 2001.
Karlyn Bowman	"College Students' Attitudes," *American Enterprise*, September 2002.
Ruth Conniff	"Patriot Games," *Progressive*, January 2002.
Don Feder and Kirkpatrick Sale	"Symposium: Is a Renewal of Patriotism Necessary for America's Survival?" *Insight on the News*, June 4, 2001.
Loyd Grossman	"Why We Love the Flag and the Frontier," *New Statesman*, December 17, 2001.
Lee Harris	"The Intellectual Origins of America-Bashing," *Policy Review*, December 2002–January 2003.
Larry Hufford	"United States Today Needs Patriotism, Not Nationalism," *National Catholic Reporter*, October 18, 2002.
Wendy Kaminer	"Patriotic Dissent," *American Prospect*, November 5, 2001.
Michael Kazin	"A Patriotic Left," *Dissent*, Fall 2002.
Thomas J. McCarthy	"On Being a Patriot," *America*, September 16, 2002.
Bill Moyers	"Which America Will We Be Now?" *Nation*, November 19, 2001.
Ched Myers	"Mixed Blessing," *Other Side*, January/February 2002.
Cecilia O'Leary and Tony Platt	"Pledging Allegiance: The Revival of Prescriptive Patriotism," *Social Justice*, Fall 2001.
Matthew Rothschild	"The New McCarthyism," *Progressive*, January 2002.
Sam Smith	"How to Be a Patriot," *Yes! A Journal of Positive Futures*, Spring 2002.
U.S. News & World Report	"Patriotism's Exquisite Privileges," June 3, 2002.

CHAPTER 4

How Can American Values Be Improved?

Chapter Preface

In examining ways to reinforce and enhance values that most Americans consider essential to a democratic nation, policy makers have lately focused on public school curricula. In February 1993, for example, a national coalition known as the Character Education Partnership (CEP) was founded to help communities across the United States implement values education in their schools. CEP hopes to instill in students "good character," which they define as understanding, caring about, and acting on core ethical values. These core values, according to CEP, include honesty, responsibility, fairness, trustworthiness, caring, respect, and hard work.

Two significant events in the late 1990s spurred greater public interest in values education, also referred to as character education. In 1998, a poll conducted by the Josephson Institute of Ethics found that nearly seven out of ten high school students had cheated on a test at least once during the previous year. The same survey also found that nearly half of all high school students had shoplifted. Then in 1999, a shooting spree at Columbine High School in Littleton, Colorado, left fifteen dead, including two student gunmen. This incident, the deadliest case of school violence in U.S. history, convinced many experts that the claims about escalating youth violence and declining morals were true, and it resulted in increased calls for character education programs. As CEP chair Sanford M. McDonnell argues, "Too many young people are growing up with almost no exposure to the values upon which our freedom is based. . . . It is the schools that have the greatest potential for overcoming this national crisis of character."

To date, thousands of school districts have adopted character education. Some programs incorporate intensive history courses and discussions on controversial topics to foster democratic ideals and moral understanding. Other programs encourage moral reflection across the curriculum, with teachers instilling core values through the study of science, literature, and social studies. Still others focus on inspiring a sense of responsibility and community through school assemblies, homeroom discussions, and volunteer activities.

However, not everyone welcomes the spread of character education. Critics warn that public schools could use character education to promote values contrary to parents' beliefs. Both conservatives and liberals are concerned about what track character educators might take when faced with controversial issues such as abortion, sex education, and homosexuality. Even discussing seemingly noncontroversial values, such as tolerance and justice, could be problematic. As commentator David Carlin asks, "Will the schools teach liberal or conservative values? Values of self-expression or self-control? Values rooted in religion or in secularism?" Others question whether it is wise to allow state institutions to teach morality. A reader responding to a *New York Times Magazine* article on character education wrote, "Do you suppose that if [Nazi] Germany had had character education . . . it would have encouraged children to fight Nazism or support it?"

Character education is just one among many strategies for enhancing American values. In the following chapter, authors debate several other proposals for improving America's moral climate, including conservative social and family policies, the promotion of altruism, and state-supported displays of religious items.

| *"Marriage-strengthening efforts by the government are urgently needed today with family breakdown rampant in America."*

Policies That Favor the Traditional Family Strengthen American Values

Bridget Maher

In the following viewpoint Bridget Maher asserts that marriage and the traditional two-parent family should be seen as crucial ingredients in America's system of values. According to Maher, marriage curbs abortion, domestic violence, drug abuse, poverty, and teen premarital sex. Alternatives to marriage—such as single parenthood, cohabitation, and homosexual relationships—have detrimental effects and should be discouraged, claims Maher. The government should work to conserve and promote marriage, she concludes, because it is the primary building block of society and the foundation of a strong nation. Maher is a marriage and family policy analyst at the Family Research Council, a think tank based in Washington, D.C.

As you read, consider the following questions:

1. According to Maher, single women are responsible for what percentage of abortions?
2. How does divorce affect children, according to the author?
3. Why is cohabitation a poor environment in which to raise children, in Maher's opinion?

A lthough the decision to marry someone is private, marriage itself is not a private act. Marriage is, in fact, the most important social act, one that involves more than just the married couple. Extended families are merged and renewed through a wedding. It is also through marriage that the community and the nation are renewed. A new home is formed when a couple marries, one open to the creation of new life. These children are the future. Marriage also has beneficial social and health effects for both adults and children, and these gifts benefit the community and the whole society. Conversely, it is through the breakdown of marriage that society is gravely harmed. The future of the nation depends on the creation of good marriages and good homes for children.

Common sense and an overwhelming amount of social science data show that children raised by their biological married parents have the best chance of becoming happy, healthy, responsible, morally-upright citizens. Children with married parents are much safer than children living in single-parent homes. They are less likely to be aborted and less likely to be abused or neglected. Children in intact families also have better emotional health and engage in fewer risky behaviors, including substance abuse and delinquency. Premarital sex and having children out of wedlock are also less common among children in intact families. Moreover, children with married parents fare better economically and experience greater educational success than do those with unmarried parents.

Marriage also positively affects adults, as married people are more likely to be healthy, productive, and engaged citizens. They have better emotional and physical health and live longer than do unmarried people. Moreover, married couples have greater incomes than do single adults, and the longer they stay married, the more wealth they accumulate. Marriage particularly benefits men's earnings capacities. As sociologist Steven Nock's research demonstrates, "Once married, men earn more, work more, and have better jobs."

Protecting Human Life

Less abortion. The benefits of marriage greatly impact society. Marriage helps human life to be protected and cherished, as married women are less likely to abort their children than are unmarried women. More than 80 percent of abortions are obtained by single women. Abortion makes human beings seem like disposable products, able to be killed if they are unwanted, and it has opened the door to stem cell research, cloning, euthanasia, and assisted suicide. With fewer abortions, human life is more likely to be respected at all stages: from tiny, defenseless embryo to frail, disabled elderly person. It also means that fewer women will be harmed physically and emotionally by abortion. Millions of women have suffered serious post-abortion effects, including depression, anxiety, cervical damage, excessive bleeding, and sterility. Marriage, then, will help to protect both women and children.

Safer Homes. Marriage makes homes safer places to live because it curbs social problems such as domestic violence, which is much more common among cohabitants than among spouses. In a 2002 study, cohabiting couples reported physical aggression in their relationships at rates three times higher than those reported by married couples. Also, divorced and separated women have the highest rates of violent abuse by a spouse, ex-spouse, or boyfriend. Not only does marriage help ensure women's safety, it also helps to defray the social costs of domestic violence. According to a 1999 study, annual medical costs for abused women are about $1.8 billion, a figure which does not include costs for shelters, lost wages and productivity, and other non-medical expenses.

Marriage also helps to curb child abuse, which is more common among single-parent families compared to married-parent families. A 1996 national study on child abuse found that children in single-parent families had a 77 percent greater risk of harm by physical abuse and an 87 percent greater risk of harm due to physical neglect than did children living in two-parent homes. With less child abuse and neglect, more children can enjoy the security and love of married parents, rather than languish in the foster care system, which is a very expensive government program. . . .

The Social Gifts of Marriage

Safer communities. Communities with more married-parent families will also be safer and better places to live, because they are less likely to have substance abuse and crime among young people. Married parents are more likely to provide the security and supervision their children need, thus discouraging them from substance abuse and crime. A 1999 study of more than 4,000 youth found that those who experience one or more changes in family structure during adolescence were at much greater risk for drug abuse and delinquency. A 1998 Department of Justice report reveals that six out of ten jail inmates in the U.S. were raised by a single parent or neither parent. Drug abuse and crime are likely to lead to other negative behaviors, including poor performance in school, premarital sex, addiction, and violence. . . .

With more married-parent families, not only are drug abuse and criminal justice costs much lower, but communities are safer and more young people will enjoy a greater likelihood of finishing school and growing up to be productive, intelligent adults. . . .

The Renewal of the Traditional Family

Can the family survive in the 21st century? "Yes," in the long-term sense that the family is natural, meaning that it is rooted in human nature. No matter how many distortions in ideas or practice that we impose on the family, it has the capacity to bounce back. Because it is *natural*, the family is capable of this renewal. It may occur in a corrupted society that is shocked back to its senses. Renewal may occur through the coming of a new generation of young, who reject the follies of their elders. Or it may occur through another, more vital people moving in to displace the dissipated remnants of a population who thought they no longer needed the family, but renewal it will be.

Allan Carlson, *The Family in America*, December 2001.

Less premarital sex and unwed childbearing. Marriage helps to prevent premarital sex among young people, since those raised with married parents are less likely to have sex before marriage, compared to those raised in single-parent or step-families. With less premarital sex, there are fewer out-of-wedlock births, which greatly benefits society, since children born out of wedlock are likely to be delinquent, abuse drugs, and engage in premarital sex. Fewer out-of-wedlock births also help to prevent poverty and welfare dependence, as unwed parents are often poor. . . .

Another result of reducing premarital sex would be fewer sexually transmitted diseases (STDs), which are rampant among the young: two-thirds of new cases of STDs occur in young people between the ages of 15 and 24. A decline in sexually transmitted diseases not only means healthier young people, but also less infertility and cervical cancer as well as fewer medical costs. The Human Papillomavirus (HPV), the most common STD, is found in 99.7 percent of cervical cancers. Annual medical costs for treating STDs and their complications among Americans were $8.4 billion in 1996, which does not include non-medical costs such as lost wages and productivity as well as expenses resulting from STDs passed on to infants.

Marriage and Civic Responsibility

More marriage and less divorce. Along with reducing social problems, married-parent homes are more likely to produce young adults who view marriage positively and maintain life-long marriages. Divorce, on the other hand, is likely to breed more divorce and often contributes to cohabitation and negative attitudes toward marriage. According to a 2001 study, children from divorced homes are twice as likely to divorce as are children from intact homes. Also, in an effort to avoid divorce, children from divorced homes often cohabit before marriage, making them at higher risk for marital breakup than those who do not live together. Moreover, compared to those raised in intact families, adults who had experienced parental divorce are less likely to agree that marriage is better than living as a single person, that marriage is a life-long commitment, and that children are better off living in an intact family. . . .

More involved citizens. Married adults are more likely to engage in civic activities, such as voting and community involvement. A 2002 study found that "married adults were 1.3 times more likely than unmarried adults to have volunteered [to perform social service], and married adults averaged 1.4 times more volunteer hours than unmarried individuals." Also parents were almost twice as likely as those without children to volunteer in social service projects. Another 2002 study found that compared to single parents, married parents know more about their neighbors, and are more likely to participate in civic and school organizations and to bring their children to church. Marriage, it appears, creates more vital communities, in which people look after one another and take seriously their responsibilities as citizens.

The Government's Role in Strengthening Marriage

Government can legitimately privilege marriage and seek to strengthen it through public policy, because marriage serves public purposes: namely, procreation and the benefit of children and society. Other relationships, such as cohabitation and homosexuality, do not benefit children and society—as a result, they should not be supported by government. There is no evidence showing that these relationships have the same positive effects as marriage. In fact, there is considerable evidence that they have detrimental effects on both children and adults.

Cohabiting Households

Four out of ten cohabiting households have children, but children in these homes are likely to fare poorly: they are more likely to have emotional and behavioral problems—such as not getting along with peers, difficulty with concentration, and feeling depressed—compared to children with married biological parents. Also, children living with cohabiting adults are more likely to do poorly academically and to live in poverty. Moreover, children in cohabiting households are likely to experience the breakup of their parents or parent and partner. A 2000 study found that, in a given year, only 46 percent of cohabiting couples said they are definitely planning to marry their partner, however, five to seven years later, only 52 percent of these couples were married and 31 percent were no longer cohabiting. Cohabiting couples who marry are likely to have communication problems, low levels of commitment to marriage, and a high risk of divorce. According to a 1992 study, couples who cohabited before marriage were 46 percent more likely to divorce than were married couples who did not first cohabit.

Cohabitation is not a good environment for raising children. Lack of commitment among cohabitants sets a bad example for children, teaching them that premarital sex, having children out of wedlock, and cohabitation are appropriate behaviors. Also, domestic violence is much more common among cohabiting households, creating an unsafe environment for children. Moreover, due to the instability of their relationships, cohabitants have a much higher incidence of depression, affecting parents' emotional availability. Married parents give children a much more stable and safe home.

Homosexual and Lesbian Households

Homosexual couples cannot procreate, but some of them choose to adopt children. However, homosexual households are often unstable and full of disease, domestic violence and depression, rendering them incapable of providing a secure and wholesome environment for raising children. Homosexuals are likely to practice risky sexual behaviors, such as anal intercourse and promiscuity, which often lead to sexually transmitted diseases (STDs) such as AIDS and Human Papillomavirus (HPV). According to the Centers for Disease Control, a majority of the cumulative AIDS cases in the United States have been in men who have sex with men (some of whom also inject drugs, an added risk factor). Even homosexuals in "monogamous" relationships are at high risk for contracting STDs, because they are likely to engage in unsafe sex more often. Hepatitis, gay bowel syndrome, and anal cancer are also prevalent among homosexual men, along with a reduced life expectancy. Lesbians are at risk for sexually transmitted diseases and have high rates of alcohol abuse, while both homosexuals and lesbians have high rates of domestic violence, depression, suicide, and molestation of children.

Along with living in a harmful environment, children in homosexual or lesbian households are denied the benefits of having a married mother and father. They are unable to experience the unique, complementary roles of a man and a woman in marriage and parenting. Also, they are likely to imitate the behavior of their parents; studies have shown that children raised in homosexual and lesbian households are more likely to engage in sexual experimentation and homosexual behavior as adults. Only a man and a woman united in marriage can provide children with the proper role models, stability, and attention they need.

Restoring a Culture of Marriage

Marriage-strengthening efforts by the government are urgently needed today with family breakdown rampant in America. The marriage rate is at an all-time low, while the divorce rate is twice that of 1960. More than one million children annually experience their parents' divorce, and they are likely to have long-lasting emotional scars and to suffer academically and economically. Also, the number of cohabiting couples has increased dramatically during the past 30 years: in 2000, there were 5.5 million cohabiting households, compared to just 500,000 in 1970. Today, one-third of all births are out of wedlock. Although the teen birthrate declined during the 1990s, there were 1.35 million out-of-wedlock births in 2001. . . .

All citizens, including policymakers, should do their part to uphold the institution of marriage, because it provides the best environment for raising children, who are the future of our society. Strengthening marriage creates a stronger foundation for the family, the basic social building block, and produces a stronger nation that benefits many future generations. Unfortunately, marriage has been badly weakened by decades of divorce, out-of-wedlock childbearing and cohabitation. America needs to restore a culture of marriage in which monogamous, life-long marriages are the norm, and marriage between a man and a woman is treasured as the safest and best haven for children. Pro-marriage policies—as well as community and church marriage-strengthening efforts—will contribute to shaping such a culture.

"[The conservative agenda is] not my moral vision of liberty, or justice, for all."

Policies That Favor the Traditional Family Threaten American Values

Wendy Kaminer

According to Wendy Kaminer in the following viewpoint, the right-wing marriage movement claims that the family is the foundation of a stable society, yet it would deny gay couples the right to wed, thereby increasing instability. Conservatives would also limit the right to divorce and undercut reproductive choice, notes Kaminer. Such restrictions on the family contradict the conservative principle of minimal government interference in private life, the author points out; they also exemplify a kind of moralism that is opposed to freedom and justice. Kaminer is a lawyer, social critic, reporter, and writer who serves on the national board of the American Civil Liberties Union.

As you read, consider the following questions:
1. In Kaminer's view, what proves that the conservative drive to promote marriage is not purely pragmatic?
2. What are covenant marriages, according to the author?
3. Married couples with children constitute what percent of American households, according to Kaminer?

Wendy Kaminer, "Law and Marriage," *The American Prospect*, vol. 12, July 2, 2001, p. 29. Copyright © 2001 by The American Prospect, Inc. All rights reserved. Reproduced with permission from *The American Prospect*, 5 Broad St., Boston, MA 02109.

These days I settle for small and subtle signs of progress. Take the story in the February 15, [2001], *Washington Post* on the demise of a proposal in the Virginia legislature that would have required public-school students to recite the Pledge of Allegiance. State Senator Warren E. Barry—the outraged sponsor of the legislation, which was amended by his senate colleagues—blamed "libertarians and liberals" on the education committee of Virginia's house of representatives for softening his bill by exempting students who had a religious or philosophical objection to reciting the pledge. Withdrawing the defanged bill in protest, Barry called the 23 members of the committee "spineless pinkos," which, the *Post* felt compelled to explain, is "a Cold War reference to Communist sympathizers." Surely we've progressed a little if a phrase like "spineless pinkos" has passed out of the vernacular.

A Return to the 1950s?

Still, the culture of the 1950s remains appealing to some. "It may be the twenty-first century out there, but in this house it's 1954," Tony Soprano reminded his daughter on the HBO series *The Sopranos*. It's not hard to imagine social conservatives nodding their heads in agreement (though many of them consider the popularity of *The Sopranos* another sign of civilization's decline). If newly empowered right-wing moralists prevail, it may soon be 1954 in everybody's house.

What's most alluring to conservatives about the culture of the 1950s are the marriage myths it helped perpetuate. My grade school readers were replete with pictures of contented suburban, two-parent families: They lived behind white picket fences and attended church on Sunday; the women wore dresses and high heels at home. You can measure the divide between feminists and traditionalists by the way they react to this vision of bliss. Feminists tend to prefer a 50 percent divorce rate to the feminine mystique that accompanied prefeminist notions of marital stability. Traditionalists view divorce as a primary social ill, quite literally.

"Married people live longer and healthier lives," according to newspaper columnist Maggie Gallagher, co-author with Linda J. Waite of *The Case for Marriage*. A spokeswoman for the right-wing marriage movement, Gallagher imagines that marriage "wards off death" because it promotes healthier habits: Married people are "less likely to hang out late at night in bars, get into fights, drink too much, or drive too fast. They save money and pay their bills, responsibly, reducing financial stresses that undercut health." She doesn't add that married people are a lot more likely to commit adultery. Hasn't she ever been accosted by a drunken married man who was hanging out late at night in a bar?

Or are philandering spouses mere anomalies? According to Gallagher, married persons have less incentive to loiter late in bars because "to top it off, they even have better sex, more often, than couples who are not married." Maybe so— though the sexual satisfaction of married couples may owe something to the high divorce rate.

Conservative Anxiety

But let's agree that people do derive many personal as well as economic benefits from amicable, stable marriages. If the drive to strengthen marriage were pragmatic, as Gallagher makes it seem, there'd be much less opposition to gay marriages. Surely gay people and their children would also benefit from wedded bliss, or at least wedded stability, and society would benefit in turn. But while social-issue conservatives rally around calls for marriage education in public schools and for laws severely restricting divorce, they rally against legislation that would give gay couples equal rights to wed (or to work—they also oppose equal-employment laws). "Homosexuality is a permanent, defining issue" for the Christian right, Frederick Clarkson observes in the *Public Eye*, the informative magazine of Political Research Associates.

Moralism, not a pragmatic concern for health and welfare, drives the marriage movement. The conservative crusade to promote marriage exemplifies the antilibertarianism of the right, exposing the hypocrisy of its demands for smaller government and professed disdain for social engineering. The Heritage Foundation has proposed establishing a federal "marriage office" and various states are experimenting with their own forms of bureaucratic interference with private life. Arizona, Arkansas, and Louisiana recognize covenant marriages: prenuptial agreements that greatly restrict the right to divorce. (Arkansas is in the midst of a "marital emergency," according to its governor, Mike Huckabee.) Divorce rates are particularly high in several Bible Belt states, including Arkansas and Oklahoma—which has budgeted $10 million for marriage counseling and has hired "marriage ambassadors" to visit talk shows and schools; May 5 [2001] was "Save Your Marriage before It Starts Day" for Oklahomans. Florida requires high schools to offer classes in marriage and relationships, and many state legislatures are considering laws that would mandate counseling before marriage or divorce.

Family Diversity Is Here to Stay

It is time to face the irreversible historical fact that family diversity is here to stay. Of course, two good parents of whatever gender generally are better than one. But no one lives in a "general" family. Our unique, often imperfect, real families assume many shapes, sizes, and characters. Each type of family has strengths, vulnerabilities, and challenges, and each needs support and deserves respect. We can't coerce or preach people into successful marital or parenting relationships, but we can help them to succeed in the ones they form. What we need to promote instead of divisive self-righteous family values are inclusive, democratic, and compassionate *social* values.

Judith Stacey, *Utne Reader*, September/October 1996.

Conservative anxiety about marriage reflected by these measures has been heightened by recently released census figures showing that fewer than 24 percent of American households consist of married couples with kids. Meanwhile, the percentage of families headed by single mothers has risen 25 percent in the past 10 years. "We're losing; there isn't any question about it" virtuecrat William Bennett warns.

Right-Wing Moralism

It's not surprising that the crusade to reverse these trends by promoting traditional heterosexual marriage and restricting divorce coincides with a retreat from feminist campaigns for freedom and economic equality. While considering proposals for a federal marriage office, the Bush administration has closed the White House Office for Women's Initiatives and Outreach, which served as a liaison for women's advocacy groups. The president has appointed staunch antifeminist opponents of affirmative action to top economic and labor jobs (although he himself is a deft practitioner of affirmative action, as his cabinet and court appointments show). He moved quickly to curtail abortion rights—and even speech about abortion—by reinstituting a ban on abortion counseling by international family-planning organizations that receive U.S. funding. Other anti-choice initiatives will be more subtle: The proposed federal marriage office would redirect some family-planning funding to teen-abstinence programs.

Liberals routinely condemn advocates of abstinence programs or covenant marriages for trying to "legislate morality" but law and policy are naturally moralistic. Equal-employment laws are not simply pragmatic economic measures; they reflect a consensus about the immorality of discrimination—a consensus that liberals fought hard to create. Workplace regulations in general—minimum wage laws and health-and-safety regulations—are considered moral mandates by many on the left. Hate-crime legislation and campus speech codes all reflect the left's moralism; so do efforts to abolish the death penalty and to end the deeply immoral war on drugs. So attacking right-wing moralism can be a bit misleading, if not downright hypocritical.

I have no quarrel with efforts to use law to promote morality; that's partly what it's for. I do object fiercely to the particular moral code that the right embraces. (I'm not always in agreement with left-wing moralists, either, especially when they seek to limit speech.) The current regime envisions an ideal world in which heterosexual couples can't divorce and gay couples can't marry, women cannot get an abortion, and even contraception is scarce, especially for teens. Seriously ill people risk being imprisoned for using marijuana to relieve pain and nausea and maybe even to prolong their lives. Poor people are imprisoned and killed by the state without ever receiving fair trials. Children will recite the Pledge of Allegiance, or else. It's not my moral vision of liberty, or justice, for all.

"[Should citizens] work for the common good rather than simply for their own private welfare?"

A Commitment to the Common Good Enhances American Values

Larry Parks Daloz

Larry Parks Daloz is coauthor of *Common Fire: Leading Lives of Commitment in a Complex World* and an associate director of the Whidbey Institute, an interfaith educational organization located on Whidbey Island, Washington. In the viewpoint that follows, Daloz maintains that a genuine commitment to the common good is essential in an increasingly complex and diverse nation. Those who work for the benefit of others recognize the significance of human connectedness and refuse to become numb to the suffering of others, writes Daloz. This empathy facilitates dialogue between communities, encourages critical thinking, and fosters hope for the future, he concludes.

As you read, consider the following questions:
1. According to the author, why did social activist Dorothy Day decline the label of saint?
2. How can an awareness of one's own pain lead to compassion, in Daloz's opinion?
3. In Daloz's view, what can help people develop the ability to recognize injustice?

Larry Parks Daloz, "Common Fire," *Yes! A Journal of Positive Futures*, Fall 1999, pp. 31–33. Copyright © 1999 by Positive Futures Network. Reproduced by permission.

Do what you love. Know your own bone; gnaw at it, bury it, unearth it, and gnaw at it still. Do not be too moral. You may cheat yourself out of much life so. Aim above morality. Be not simply good—be good for something.

—Henry David Thoreau

There are millions of citizens who refuse to succumb to what their more cynical neighbors call "reality," who insist with their lives that there has to be a better way—and who day by day go about bringing it into being. What makes them tick? What enables them to see beneath the surface and work for the common good rather than simply for their own private welfare? What inspires people to act from their own sense of a larger integrity even when it means going contrary to the status quo? And how can these circles of compassion widen?

Wondering about these questions, Sharon Parks, Cheryl and James Keen, and I listened to the stories of 145 educators, entrepreneurs, homemakers, youth workers, artists, attorneys, writers, scientists, religious leaders, and physicians who are working to improve schools, health, business practices, race relations, economic conditions—the quality of public life in general. Some were well-known and well-paid, others little-known and underpaid. Representing a range of religions, ethnicities, and social classes, all were doing tough and complex work on behalf of the common good; they were aware of how their work related to the larger economic, social, and political system, and had been steadily committed for at least a decade. What patterns characterize their lives? What keeps them going in the face of discouragement? The full story appears in our book, *Common Fire: Leading Lives of Commitment in a Complex World*, but here is some of what we learned.

Normal and Healthy People

In a world that assumes fundamental human nature to be self-interested, people who work primarily on behalf of the whole commons are often labeled "saints"—or worse, martyrs or hypocrites. The great social activist Dorothy Day declined the honor, declaring that she did not wish to be called a saint because she didn't want to be "dismissed so easily." She was all too aware that saints are more admired than emulated and knew that a recognition of our fallibility is what keeps us grounded.

Although there are risks aplenty in committing oneself to the common good, people who do so rarely describe themselves as courageous. Kelly Seabrook, who works with young drug offenders in Boston's "combat zone," told us, "It's not courage; it's just where I should be." Perhaps it is not these people but our idea of what is "normal" that is out of step.

In fact, we were struck by how healthy the people we studied were. For the most part, they were raised in homes where they learned to trust that the world would work for them and where they were encouraged to make a difference. This did not mean that their families were necessarily affluent (35 percent of our sample came from poor or working-class backgrounds), nor did it mean that they had conventionally "happy childhoods." There was ample suffering to go around. But even where the immediate family failed, there was always an aunt, a grandfather, or sometimes a caring neighbor or teacher who provided the support and assurance that life could be lived more fully. Sometimes this made the vital difference between a life shattered and one healed.

A Certainty of Connection

In our highly individualistic culture, we tend to uphold a romantic vision of the altruistic hero, a lone, isolated individual who stands against the tide for what is right, indifferent to what others think. And yet few if any of those we studied represented this stereotype. Rather, they cared what others thought and felt, and were characterized by a particular capacity for connection, an ability to draw others around them into communities of comfort and challenge.

Anne Sanchez, working for years to involve disaffected citizens in the political process said, "You don't make it on your own, and in my experience, the people who tried were the people who lost their commitments." Without the knowledge that we are intrinsically connected with one another, our effectiveness is sharply limited, and we are ill-equipped for the long haul in the face of the inevitable difficulties that arise when we do have to stand up for what is right.

Under the barrage of violent media images, it's easy to become numb to the suffering of those on distant TV screens and of neighbors around the corner. Yet people committed to the common good remain open to the suffering around them, in part because they are reasonably in touch with their own pain—neither sealing it out nor being debilitated by it.

Seven Practices That Can Make a Difference

- Meet with two or three people about a public concern that troubles you—even if you don't know what to do about it. (Then arrange to meet again even if you still don't know what to do about it.)
- Make on effort to get to know someone from outside your own "tribe."
- Ask yourself regularly: Who needs me as a mentor? Who is watching how I live and the choices I make—and who needs me to affirm, challenge, and inspire them?
- Be dependable and trustworthy for the children who count on you. If you don't have children in your life, support your friends who are parents or grandparents. Families work best when there is a network of encouragement in the neighborhood and workplace.
- Avoid violent images that numb your response to genuine suffering and distract you from the true stories of our time. When you encounter suffering, let it move you to action.
- Stay alive to beauty, awe, and delight. Paying attention to wonder creates hope.
- Don't be a Lone Ranger. Find a community of comfort and challenge and invest your time and money in keeping it alive—for your own and the world's sake.

Larry Parks Daloz, *Yes! A Journal of Positive Futures*, Fall 1999.

After years of beatings at the hands of his alcoholic father, Paul Chen finally left home and was rescued by a neighborhood youth worker. He subsequently became a pastor with a deep commitment to economic justice and community building. "There's not a day that I'm not reminded of human connectedness because of the pain I share from my own background," he told us.

Sometimes, as with Chen, the personal anguish is great, but more often it is of the sort that most of us experience during the course of simply living fully. The key lies not in our suffering, but in our ability to use it to connect with the pain of others. Held poorly, our torment seals us off from others or disables us; held well, awareness of our own pain enables us to resonate with that of others and work toward the healing of the whole community.

Despite a certain truth in the bromide that "before you help others you should have it together yourself," this is often more excuse than wisdom. It's what Paul Rogat Loeb refers to as "the perfect standard," the insistence that one must be perfect, without doubt, before taking any action.

Liz Brown, a physician who works with AIDS-afflicted infants in an inner city hospital freely acknowledges that a part of her passion for children's health care lies in her inability to have children of her own. In fact, helping others and healing oneself often go hand in hand. A growing number of psychotherapists now urge their clients to take part in service activities as they heal their own wounds.

At Home in the World

In a world of growing cultural diversity, many Americans are retreating to their own "cocoons," living in gated communities, sticking together with their own kind, cultivating a world of "us" and "them." Where diversity is inevitable, it is often seen as a problem to be overcome rather than an opportunity to be welcomed. Those whom we interviewed were able to respond to the voices of the entire community, attending to those who were very different from themselves.

Indeed, the single strongest pattern was that at some point during their formative years, virtually everyone we interviewed had experienced a positive relationship with someone significantly different from themselves, of a different "tribe." Significantly, almost three quarters of our sample had traveled abroad by young adulthood.

Furthermore, the experience was more than a casual encounter; it included a felt, empathic connection, a relationship that created a deep sense of the fundamental humanity of the other.

When Tracy Flanagan was a teen, a conflict broke out between the Black and White kids in her neighborhood. The local priest tapped Tracy to help mediate.

Although she became a lightning rod for the anger of both

sides, she emerged stronger for the experience. Over the subsequent years, she became increasingly involved in such "cross-tribal" experiences. Today she is the director of a fair-housing agency in a major urban area. It is encounters like hers that transform the "us" and "them" into a "we"—the ground of commitment to the common good.

It's the System . . .

At a time when conventional wisdom seeks out single causes and simple answers to our complex social challenges, or when we are tempted to explain problems solely in terms of individual personality, those who sustain long-term commitment have learned to see the "systemic" dimensions of life. Where others see misfortune, they recognize injustice.

One of the most important ways in which this capacity is learned is through mentors—college teachers, job supervisors, internship leaders, senior managers, rabbis and pastors—older adults who are present at a crucial time in a young person's development, who help them to see their world in a more critically informed way, and who model a committed life themselves.

When he graduated from college, Jack Heinz went to work with a small food co-op in the mid-west. The director soon became a mentor for Jack, sending him to a United Nations conference where he came face to face with the problems of global hunger and began to see the connections between poverty and our economic system. His mentor later brought him onto the board of the organization. Over the years, Jack became increasingly involved with international development and eventually became head of one of the largest and most successful private relief agencies in the world.

Ease with Ambiguity

Few if any of those we interviewed would claim to hold "the truth" for all people, though all assert strong life-affirming values. It is as though they do not need to live with the answers all formed, nor do they expect this of others. Somehow the evolution of their lives has taught them to be at ease with mystery and the ambiguity that invariably comes with complex territory.

Interestingly, this willingness to dwell with mystery extends to the way they imagine the future as well. Such people are often thought of as "visionaries," and yet when asked what their vision is, more often than not they demur, saying that the vision must be created by the whole community they are working with. Their notion of leadership is to bring forth a shared vision rather than to articulate their own and expect others to follow.

"It's not a vision so much as a process," said one person, adding, "but you have to be clear about the broad values."

In the final analysis one must also be clear about what one needs to flourish as a committed human being. When we asked Valerie Russell, a veteran civil rights worker who had faced down the dogs and the billy clubs, how she managed to stay the course, especially when it got discouraging, she responded immediately: "Meals and music."

We heard others speak similarly. Meals shared together with a few friends and colleagues provide the nourishment for body and spirit that comes from a combination of good food and good conversation—conversation that gives perspective, heals, and helps us to say "yes" all over again. And music can help us hold it all together—the suffering and the wonder of life itself—in a way that anchors and re-invigorates the soul. How we are together and what feeds our souls is what finally makes the difference in a world hungry for hope.

| *"The implicit basis of American government was an ethics of individualism—the view that the individual is not subordinate to the collective."*

A Commitment to the Common Good Endangers American Values

Robert Tracinski

Robert Tracinski is a senior fellow at the Ayn Rand Institute in Irvine, California. The institute promotes the philosophy of Ayn Rand, author of *Atlas Shrugged* and *The Fountainhead*. In the following viewpoint Tracinski denounces the concept of altruism, arguing that a commitment to the common good contradicts the ethic of independence and individualism upon which America was founded. In fact, Tracinski points out, Nazi morality was rooted in the notion that the individual should make sacrifices for the larger community. This misguided form of idealism opposes the American principle that each individual has a right to life, liberty, and the pursuit of happiness, the author asserts.

As you read, consider the following questions:
1. What was Hitler's view on the individual ego, according to Tracinski?
2. In the author's opinion, what are some possible consequences of altruistic self-sacrifice?
3. What did the Founding Fathers do to protect against the "tyranny of the majority," according to Tracinski?

Robert Tracinski, "Why It Can Happen Again," *MediaLink*, April 22, 2003.

On Holocaust Remembrance Day, we are urged to memorialize the millions who suffered and died in the Nazi concentration camps. The purpose is not merely to pay tribute to the victims, but to learn what made an evil of such magnitude possible—to prevent it from ever happening again.

Yet this is precisely what we have failed to learn. The rise of Nazism is often attributed to such non-fundamental factors as the resentment produced by the Versailles Treaty or the despair generated by the Great Depression. Or, if we are given a fundamental, ideological explanation, we are told that the Germans had embraced too much capitalism and individualism.

The Moral Foundations of Nazism

The actual cause of Nazism was ideological—but exactly the opposite ideology. Nazism flourished because of its ethics of self-abnegation and self-sacrifice. Hitler himself stated the moral foundations of Nazism:

"It is thus necessary that the individual should finally come to realize that his own ego is of no importance. . . . This state of mind, which subordinates the interests of the ego to the conservation of the community, is really the first premise for every truly human culture. . . . The basic attitude from which such activity arises, we call—to distinguish it from egoism and selfishness—idealism. By this we understand only the individual's capacity to make sacrifices for the community, for his fellow men."

Historians usually dismiss such statements. The idea that self-sacrifice is synonymous with virtue is too uncontroversial for them to connect to Nazism. Thus, such pronouncements are usually regarded as mere window dressing to disguise the Nazis' true agenda.

But what if this view is wrong? What if it was precisely the Nazis' most virtuous-sounding slogans that unleashed their evil on the world?

Altruism Is Servitude

Consider the full, logical meaning of altruistic self-sacrifice. It means, not benevolence toward others, but servitude. If sacrifice to others is the essence of virtue, how can anyone be allowed to pursue his own goals and happiness? If the community needs money, it is the individual's duty to sacrifice his earnings. If society decides that certain ideas are dangerous, it is the individual's duty to sacrifice his beliefs. And if the nation decrees that certain individuals are dangerous, then they must be sacrificed. The needs of the collective, not the interests and the rights of the individual, become the standard of right and wrong.

Not the Message of America

What we hear from politicians, intellectuals, and the media is that independence is passé, that we've reached a new age of "interdependence." We hear demands for mandatory "volunteering" to serve others, for sacrifice to the nation. We hear demands from trust-busters that successful companies be punished for being "greedy" and not serving society. But this is not the message of America. It is the direct opposite of why America became a beacon of hope for the truly oppressed throughout the world. They have come here to escape poverty and dictatorship; they have come here to live their own lives, where they aren't owned by the state, the community, or the tribe.

Michael Berliner, www.aynrand.org, June 26, 2002.

Under such a philosophy, no one can complain when the Nazis freeze workers' wages—the nation needs less costly tanks. No one can speak out when Hitler arrests his political opponents—the nation needs greater unity. And no one can resist when the Jews are tortured and murdered—the nation needs Aryan purity. As Leonard Peikoff writes in *The Ominous Parallels*—a study of the philosophic similarities between America today and pre-Nazi Germany: "The opponents of Nazism were disarmed; since they equated selflessness with virtue, they could not avoid conceding that Nazism, however misguided, was a form of moral idealism."

Most people avoid these stark implications by retreating to a compromise between self-sacrifice and self-interest. Calls for sacrifice are proper, they say, but should not be taken "too far." The Fascists condemned this approach as hypocrisy. They took the morality of sacrifice to its logical conclusion. They insisted, in the words of Italian Fascist Al-

179

fredo Rocco, on "the necessity, for which the older doctrines make little allowance, of sacrifice, even up to the total immolation of individuals."

And the Nazis certainly practiced what Rocco preached. A central goal of the concentration camps, wrote survivor Bruno Bettelheim, was "to break the prisoners as individuals, and to change them into a docile mass." "There are to be no more private Germans," one Nazi writer declared; "each is to attain significance only by his service to the state." The goal of National Socialism was the relentless sacrifice of the individual: the sacrifice of his mind, his independence, and ultimately his person.

The Basis of Freedom

A free country is based on precisely the opposite principle. To protect against what they called the "tyranny of the majority," America's Founding Fathers upheld the individual's right to "life, liberty, and the pursuit of happiness." The implicit basis of American government was an ethics of individualism—the view that the individual is not subordinate to the collective, that he has a moral right to his own interests, and that all rational people benefit under such a system.

Today, however, self-sacrifice is regarded as self-evidently good. True, most people do not want a pure, consistent system of sacrifice, as practiced by the Nazis. But once the principle is accepted, no amount of this "virtue" can ever be condemned as "too much."

We will not have learned the lessons of the Holocaust until we completely reject this sacrifice-worship and rediscover the morality of individualism.

"The Ten Commandments are an integral part of the foundation of American law."

The Ten Commandments Should Be Publicly Displayed

Justin Dyer

In August 2001 Alabama judge Roy Moore stirred controversy by placing a monument carved with the Ten Commandments in a public courthouse. In 2003, under charges that this display of the Ten Commandments was unconstitutional, the monument was removed. In the viewpoint that follows, Justin Dyer argues that the Ten Commandments have shaped American law and American values and thus should be displayed in public. Moreover, he points out, if all documents containing references to God were considered unconstitutional, then famous texts like the Declaration of Independence or the Gettysburg Address must also be banned from the public square. Dyer is a freelance writer.

As you read, consider the following questions:
1. According to Dyer, what religious statement is contained in Oklahoma's preamble to its state constitution?
2. What is the intention of the American Civil Liberties Union, in the author's opinion?
3. What decorates the wall of the Supreme Court chambers, according to Dyer?

M oses is doing back flips in his grave right now, and [actor] Charlton Heston is polishing his Colt M16 assault rifle.

And let me tell you: They're pissed.

They have reason to be. Nearly 3,200 years after Moses came down from Mount Sinai—and a half a century after Charlton Heston did[1]—public displays of the Ten Commandments in America are being treated like lepers in Galilee.

Right now, there are literally dozens of lawsuits attacking the constitutionality of their display. And surprisingly, the Supreme Court is not rushing in to take any of these cases.

Maybe the Court has decided that it has had enough controversy. Or maybe they just realize what a messy issue it is.

If the Court would decide that the Ten Commandments have no legitimate secular purpose, they would be paving the way for guys like Michael Newdow to effectively make atheism America's first federally established religion.

On the other hand, if they decided in favor of the Ten Commandments displays, they would surely be disappointing their buddies over at the *New York Times* editorial board.

It's a tough decision.

Important to America

But, honestly, what is so threatening about the Ten Commandments? Save the Declaration of Independence and the Constitution, no other single document has had a more far-reaching impact on American life.

Is there anyone who would dispute that this country has deep cultural and historical roots imbedded in a theistic foundation of government? And is there anyone who would dispute the fact that the Ten Commandments are an integral part of the foundation of American law? We know this well in Oklahoma. The preamble to our state Constitution makes the connection between God and law quite nicely, concluding that we are "Invoking the guidance of Almighty God, in order to secure and perpetuate the blessings of liberty. . . ." But some people just don't like that idea. It scares them, even offends them. Forsaking logic and reason, they presume that

---

1. a reference to Heston's portrayal of Moses in the 1956 movie *The Ten Commandments*

Stayskal. © 2003 by Wayne Stayskal. Reproduced by permission.

morality and ethics, even law itself, is possible without regard for where any of it came from.

Such a blatant contempt for religion, for Judaism and Christianity, and for America's heritage is obvious in a recent district court's decision that a Ten Commandments display in the rotunda of the Alabama Judicial Building is unconstitutional.

They might as well just call Congress, the Declaration of Independence, the Gettysburg Address, money, and the Constitution unconstitutional, too.

But I'm sure all of those things are on the American Civil Liberties Union's list of things to do.

Destroying America doesn't happen over night, you know.

For now, one of their top priorities is to convince the Supreme Court to take on one of the Ten Commandment cases and then rule that their display on any public property is unconstitutional.

In the meantime, this nation's highest legislative body will continue to convene its meetings with the words "God save this honorable Court." After such, they will sit on their benches and look out at the carving of Moses and the tablets that adorn the wall of the Supreme Court chambers.

"The appropriate place for the Ten Commandments to be etched is on the heart, not on a hunk of granite ensconced in a public courthouse."

The Ten Commandments Should Not Be Publicly Displayed

J.R. Labbe

In the following viewpoint J.R. Labbe responds to an Alabama judge's unsuccessful attempt to keep a Ten Commandments monument in a public courthouse. In Labbe's opinion, true believers in the Ten Commandments recognize that they carry their faith in their hearts, not on a showcased slab of granite. Furthermore, publicly displaying the Ten Commandments with no clarifying historical context and without regard to the values of non-Christians and non-Jews violates the Constitution's prohibition on endorsing religion. Labbe is a senior editorial writer and columnist for a Texas newspaper, the *Fort Worth Star-Telegram*.

As you read, consider the following questions:

1. In Labbe's opinion, how have those who vehemently support Justice Roy Moore actually broken two of the Ten Commandments?
2. In reference to a portrayal of the Ten Commandments in the U.S. Supreme Court, what does the author mean by "context is everything"?
3. What is meant by the word "public," in Labbe's view?

W hat is it about "Thou shalt not make unto thee a graven image" that the people kneeling before 5,280 pounds of stone known as "Roy's Rock" don't get?

Perhaps those believers who gathered in the Alabama Supreme Court lobby should have opened their eyes and read the Ten Commandments before being hauled off to jail.

Graven images are a no-no. And making an idol out of a public official who compares himself to Daniel and Moses has got to evoke a heavenly tsk-tsk.

Don't misread my disappointment with people who allow their religion to be used as a political foil as disapproval of their faith or their right to express it. It's just that the appropriate place for the Ten Commandments to be etched is on the heart, not on a hunk of granite ensconced in a public courthouse.

Religion Is Not Under Attack

No one is telling Alabama Chief Justice Roy Moore, who is the choir director of this discordant hallelujah chorus, or any of his misguided followers that they can't practice their faith or acknowledge God.

As much as this scene may sound like Armageddon in Alabama, religious freedom is not under attack in America. What higher courts have said is that a monument erected in a "public" place specifically as an endorsement of religion does not pass the First Amendment test.

The Ten Commandments are displayed in the U.S. Supreme Court. But context is everything. They, along with a depiction of Moses, are part of a larger frieze that includes other historical figures of law, like Hammurabi and Confucius.

Moore has made no attempt to put his shrine in a historical context, nor have any of his supporters suggested that a plaque quoting, say, the Koran would be a welcome addition.

Supporters of the monument's continued presence in a "public" courthouse are using this issue as the platform for their broader anger over judges who have, in their estimation, turned their backs on the moral "Christian" values that made this country great. They cite, for example, the recent decision by the U.S. Supreme Court to overturn Texas' sodomy laws.

"This is not about a monument!" the Rev. Pat Mahoney,

director of the Christian Defense Coalition, shouted in network video footage from the steps of the courthouse. "This is about resisting tyranny!"

What "Public" Means

But "activist" and "tyrannical" accurately describe Moore, the "Moses of Alabama," whose defiance of higher courts' orders to remove the monument smacks of demagoguery.

Moore knew the game rules of being a "public" official when he put on those black robes. He swore an oath—something that certain branches of the Christian family would view as blasphemous—that he would uphold the Constitution of the United States. All of it.

Lowe. © 2003 by Tribune Media Services. Reproduced by permission.

Judges can't pick and choose which parts of the Constitution they want to enforce and which they want to ignore, just as Christians can't pick which commandments work for them and ignore the ones that are just too hard to keep—not unless they want to suffer damning consequences.

"Public" means that every American who walks through the

doors of that courthouse—Christian, Jew, Buddhist, Hindu, Muslim, atheist and pagan—can expect equal treatment under the law. Just as there is no religious test for the men and women who seek public office, there should be no religious test for Americans to expect justice.

No one is telling Moore that his acknowledgment of God is irrelevant when it comes to exercising justice. I imagine most people who stand before his bench pray that he will be merciful.

Seeing Things in Context

The saddest chapter of this story is the number of protesting Christians who believe that they are being persecuted, that this nation has moved away from its "Christian" roots.

Please. Being barred from reciting the Lord's Prayer over the PA system before kick-off at a public high school football game hardly ranks as persecution when in places like Sudan, Afghanistan and India, Christians are being attacked and killed because of their faith.

I repeat: Context is everything.

The apostle Paul warned that Christians would be persecuted for following Jesus. He knew whereof he spoke; he spent enough time in jail because his faith in Christ was an affront to the Roman theocracy.

But it's doubtful that Paul—the man who wrote that "every person is to be in subjection to the governing authorities" (Romans 13:1)—would have wasted his breath over a rock.

Periodical Bibliography

The following articles have been selected to supplement the diverse views presented in this chapter.

Christopher Beem — "Can Legislation Solve Our Moral Problems?" *Responsive Community*, Fall 2001.

Michael K. Briand — "Individualism and Civic Renewal," *Responsive Community*, Winter 1999–2000.

Joan Chittister — "After Great Pain: Finding a Way Out," *Christian Century*, March 22, 2003.

Joseph F. Coates — "Updating the Ten Commandments," *Futurist*, May/June 2003.

Andrew I. Cohen — "Flags, Flames, and Property," *Freeman*, January 1999.

Edd Doerr — "Jefferson's Wall . . . ," *Humanist*, January/February 2002.

Stephen Goode — "Putting Faith in the Founding Fathers," *Insight on the News*, March 4, 2003.

Krista Kafer — "How to Teach Religion in Public Schools," *World & I*, August 2002.

Stanley Kurtz — "Beyond Gay Marriage," *Weekly Standard*, August 11, 2003.

Elizabeth Lesser — "Twenty-First-Century Spirituality," *Tikkun*, January/February 2000.

Tibor R. Machan — "Self Before Others," *Free Inquiry*, Fall 2001.

Colman McCarthy, interviewed by Jon Wilson — "He'd Rather Teach Peace," *Hope*, July/August 2003.

James P. Pfiffner — "The Paradox of Governmental Power," *Society*, September 2000.

Katha Pollitt — "Stacked Decalogue," *Nation*, September 22, 2003.

Melissa Snarr — "The University of Social Justice: Beyond Community Service, Colleges Educate for Social Change," *Sojourners*, May/June 2003.

Alice Walker — "A Daring Compassion," *Yes! A Journal of Positive Futures*, Fall 1999.

For Further Discussion

Chapter 1

1. William J. Bennett defines American patriotism as the pride that U.S. citizens take in the spirit of democracy and liberty that their nation represents—and the willingness to defend those ideals. Why does Robert Jensen take issue with this notion of patriotism? After reading these viewpoints, are you more or less inclined to describe yourself as a patriot? Explain.

2. John Mueller argues that capitalism rewards honesty and virtuous business practices. Conversely, David Hilfiker asserts that capitalism fosters selfishness and greed and undermines the dignity of work. Whose argument is more persuasive, and why? Based on what you have read in these viewpoints, is capitalism beneficial for American society? Why or why not?

3. Joe Lieberman contends that American values are deeply rooted in the Judeo-Christian ethic. Dan Barker maintains that secularism and the separation of religion and state are America's defining principles. Lieberman is an Orthodox Jew; Barker is an atheist who was once a Christian minister. In what way does knowing the authors' backgrounds influence your assessment of their arguments? Explain your answer.

Chapter 2

1. Describe American teens as James A. Lee characterizes them, and as Jonathan V. Last characterizes them. Which description is more accurate, and why? Is there more reason to be negative or positive about the condition of young people in America today? Explain.

2. Both Steve Bonta and John Derbyshire have strong opinions about the state of America's popular culture. In what ways do they agree? In what ways do they disagree? Provide specific examples to support your answer.

3. Do you agree with Dolores Curran and James B. Twitchell that America is a materialistic society? Why or why not? In what way does consumerism harm society, in Curran's opinion? How does Twitchell refute the claim that consumerism is entirely negative?

Chapter 3

1. Martha C. Nussbaum maintains that feelings of patriotism can and should expand to include a sense of empathy for people of other nations. David Warren Saxe believes that too much em-

phasis on learning about other cultures actually undermines patriotism. Which author do you agree with, and why?

2. Craig Cox argues that liberal values such as a commitment to social justice and the right to dissent should be seen as patriotic. Jonah Goldberg contends that some liberal analysts have revealed themselves to be unpatriotic through their denunciations of America. Do you believe it is possible to criticize American policy and still be patriotic? Why or why not?

3. After reading the selections in this chapter, how would you define patriotism? Defend your answer with examples from the viewpoints.

Chapter 4

1. Bridget Maher maintains that the traditional, two-parent family is the foundation of a strong nation and that the government should take steps to promote marriage. How does Wendy Kaminer respond to these assertions? In your opinion, would marriage-strengthening efforts by the government be a boon to freedom, or a hindrance? Explain.

2. Based on what you have read by Larry Parks Daloz and Robert Tracinski, is altruism a feasible approach to enhancing American values? Why or why not? Are American values rooted more deeply in a commitment to the common good, or in an ethic of individualism? Give specific examples to support your claim.

3. Justin Dyer and J.R. Labbe have opposing views on whether artifacts endorsing religion should be displayed in the public square. What do you think? Do government-supported displays of religious items or beliefs violate the constitutional prohibition on state endorsement of religion? Or should such displays be viewed as a form of free speech? Explain.

Organizations to Contact

The editors have compiled the following list of organizations concerned with the issues debated in this book. The descriptions are derived from materials provided by the organizations. All have publications or information available for interested readers. The list was compiled on the date of publication of the present volume; the information provided here may change. Be aware that many organizations take several weeks or longer to respond to inquiries, so allow as much time as possible.

American Civil Liberties Union (ACLU)
125 Broad St., 18th Floor, New York, NY 10004
(212) 549-2585
Web site: www.aclu.org

The ACLU is a national organization that works to defend Americans' civil rights guaranteed in the U.S. Constitution. The ACLU publishes the quarterly newspaper *ACLU in Action* as well as the briefing papers "A History of Fighting Censorship," and "Preserving Artists' Right of Free Expression." Its Web site has a searchable archive of articles on religious liberty, students' rights, free speech, and other civil liberties issues.

American Enterprise Institute (AEI)
1150 Seventeenth St. NW, Washington, DC 20036
(202) 862-5800 • fax: (202) 862-7177
e-mail: info@aei.org • Web site: www.aei.org

The American Enterprise Institute for Public Policy Research is a scholarly research institute that is dedicated to preserving limited government, private enterprise, traditional values, and a strong national defense. It publishes a bimonthly magazine, *American Enterprise*, and *On the Issues*, a monthly compilation of articles and editorials. Reports and articles about economics, education, values, foreign policy, and other topics are available on its Web site.

Americans United for Separation of Church and State (AU)
518 C St. NE, Washington, DC 20002
(202) 466-3234 • fax: (202) 466-2587
e-mail: americansunited@au.org • Web site: www.au.org

AU works to protect the constitutional principle of church-state separation. It opposes mandatory prayer in public schools, tax dollars for parochial schools, and religious groups' participating in politics. AU publishes the monthly *Church & State* magazine as well as issue papers, legislative alerts, reference materials, and books.

The Brookings Institution
1775 Massachusetts Ave. NW, Washington, DC 20036
(202) 797-6000 • fax: (202) 797-6004
Web site: www.brookings.org

The institution, founded in 1927, is an independent think tank that conducts research and education in economics, business, government, and the social sciences. Its goal is to improve the performance of American institutions and the quality of public policy by using social science to analyze emerging issues. Its publications include the quarterly *Brookings Review*, periodic *Policy Briefs*, and books such as *America Unbound* and *Cultivating Democracy*.

Cato Institute
1000 Massachusetts Ave. NW, Washington, DC, 20001-5403
(202) 842-0200 • fax: (202) 842-3490
e-mail: cato@cato.org • Web site: www.cato.org

The Cato Institute is a libertarian public policy research foundation dedicated to limiting government and protecting individual liberties. It offers numerous publications on public policy issues, including the triennial *Cato Journal*, the bimonthly newsletter *Cato Policy Report*, and the quarterly magazine *Regulation*.

Center for the Study of Popular Culture
PO Box 67398, Los Angeles, CA 90067
(310) 843-3699 • fax: (310) 843-3692
e-mail: info@cspc.org • Web site: www.cspc.org

This educational center was started by commentators David Horowitz and Peter Collier, whose intellectual development evolved from support for the New Left in the 1960s to the forefront of today's conservatism. The center offers legal assistance and addresses many topics, including political correctness, multiculturalism, and discrimination. In 1993, the center launched a national network of lawyers called the Individual Rights Foundation to respond to the threat to First Amendment rights by college administrators and government officials. The center publishes the online *FrontPage* magazine.

Concerned Women for America (CWA)
1015 Fifteenth St. NW, Suite 1100, Washington, DC 20005
(202) 488-7000 • fax: (202) 488-0806
e-mail: mail@cwfa.org • Web site: www.cwfa.org

CWA works to strengthen marriage and the traditional family according to Judeo-Christian moral standards. It opposes abortion, pornography, feminism, and homosexuality. The organization publishes numerous brochures and policy papers as well as *Family Voice*, a monthly newsmagazine.

Council for Secular Humanism
PO Box 664, Amherst, NY 14226-0664
(716) 636-7571 • fax: (716) 636-1733
e-mail: info@secularhumanism.org
Web site: www.secularhumanism.org

The council is an educational organization dedicated to fostering the growth of democracy, secular humanism, and the principles of free inquiry. It publishes the quarterly magazine *Free Inquiry*, and its Web site includes an online library containing such articles as "Why the Christian Right Is Wrong About Homosexuality" and "Responding to the Religious Right."

Eagle Forum
PO Box 618, Alton, IL 62002
(618) 462-5415 • fax: (618) 462-8909
e-mail: eagle@eagleforum.org • Web site: www.eagleforum.org

Eagle Forum is a Christian group that promotes morality and traditional family values as revealed through a conservative interpretation of the Bible. It opposes many facets of public education and liberal government. The forum publishes the monthly *Phyllis Schlafly Report* and a periodic newsletter.

Fairness and Accuracy in Reporting (FAIR)
112 W. Twenty-seventh St., New York, NY 10001
(212) 633-6700 • fax: (212) 727-7668
e-mail: fair@fair.org • Web site: www.fair.org

FAIR is a national media watchdog group that investigates conservative bias in news coverage. Its members advocate greater diversity in the press and believe that structural reform is needed to break up the dominant media conglomerates and establish alternative, independent sources of information. *Extra!* is FAIR's bimonthly magazine of media criticism.

Family Research Council
801 G St. NW, Washington, DC 20001
(202) 393-2100 • order line: (800) 225-4008
Web site: www.frc.org

The council is a research, resource, and educational organization that promotes the traditional family, which it defines as a group of people bound by marriage, blood, or adoption. The council publishes numerous periodicals from a conservative perspective, including *Culture Facts*, a weekly report, and *Washington Watch*, a monthly newsletter. Its Web site contains an online archive of papers and publications on religion and public life, arts and culture, education, and other issues.

Freedom from Religion Foundation, Inc.

PO Box 750, Madison, WI 53701
(608) 256-8900
e-mail: ffrf@mailbag.com • Web site: www.ffrf.org

The foundation works to keep state and church separate and to educate the public about the views of freethinkers, agnostics, and nontheists. Its publications include the newspaper *Freethought Today* and the books *Losing Faith in Faith: From Preacher to Atheist* and *The Born Again Skeptic's Guide to the Bible*.

The Heritage Foundation

214 Massachusetts Ave. NE, Washington, DC 20002-4999
(202) 546-4400 • fax: (202) 546-8328
e-mail: info@heritage.org • Web site: www.heritage.org

The foundation is a public policy research institute that advocates limited government, free-market economics, individual freedom, and traditional values. Its publications include the monthly *Policy Review*, the Backgrounder series of occasional papers, and the Heritage Lecture series.

Interfaith Alliance

1331 H St. NW, 11th Floor, Washington, DC 20005
(202) 639-6370 • fax: (202) 639-6375
e-mail: tia@interfaithalliance.org
Web site: www.interfaithalliance.org

The Interfaith Alliance is a nonpartisan, clergy-led grassroots organization that advances a mainstream, faith-based political agenda. Its membership, which draws from more than fifty faith traditions, works to safeguard religious liberty, ensure civil rights, strengthen public education, and eradicate poverty. The alliance promotes religion as a healing and constructive force in public life and opposes the objectives of the religious right. It publishes the *Light*, a quarterly newsletter.

Media Research Center

325 S. Patrick St., Alexandria, VA 22314
(703) 683-9733 • (800) 672-1423 • fax: (703) 683-9736
e-mail: mrc@mediaresearch.org
Web site: www.mediaresearch.org

The center is a watchdog group that monitors liberal influence in the media. Its programs include a news division that analyzes liberal bias in mainstream news coverage. The center's publications include *Media Reality Check*, a weekly report on news stories that have been distorted or ignored, and *Flash Report*, a monthly newsletter. The Web site also offers *CyberAlert*, a daily e-mail report on national media coverage.

National Coalition Against Censorship
275 Seventh Ave., New York, NY 10001
(212) 807-6222 • fax: (212) 807-6245
e-mail: ncac@ncac.org • Web site: www.ncac.org

The coalition represents more than forty national organizations that strive to end suppression of free speech and the press. It publishes a quarterly newsletter, *Censorship News*. Other publications include the brochure "25 Years: Defending Freedom of Thought, Inquiry and Expression," and the booklet (produced in collaboration with the National Educational Association) *Public Education, Democracy, Free Speech: The Ideas That Define and Unite Us.*

National Organization for Women (NOW)
733 Fifteenth St. NW, 2nd Floor, Washington, DC 20005
(202) 628-8669 • fax: (202) 785-8576
e-mail: now@now.org • Web site: www.now.org

NOW is one of the largest and most influential feminist organizations in the United States. It seeks to end prejudice and discrimination against women in all areas of life. NOW lobbies legislatures to make laws more equitable and works to educate and inform the public on women's issues. It publishes the bimonthly paper *NOW Times*, policy statements, and articles.

People for the American Way Foundation
2000 M St. NW, Suite 400, Washington, DC 20036
(202) 467-4999 • (800) 326-7329
e-mail: pfaw@pfaw.org • Web site: www.pfaw.org

People for the American Way Foundation is a nonprofit, nonpartisan organization that opposes the political agenda of the religious right. Through public education, lobbying, and legal advocacy, the foundation defends free expression in the arts, works for equal rights for gays and lesbians, and supports public schools. The foundation's Web site includes Right Wing Watch, an online library of information about right-wing organizations, and the Progressive Network, a database with links to progressive organizations across the country.

War Resisters League (WRL)
339 Lafayette St., New York, NY 10012
(212) 228-0450 • fax: (212) 228-6193
e-mail: wrl@warresisters.org • Web site: www.warresisters.org

The WRL, founded in 1923, believes that all war is a crime against humanity and advocates nonviolent methods to create a just and democratic society. It publishes the magazine *Nonviolent Activist*. Articles from that magazine, as well as other commentary about America's war against terrorism, are available on its Web site.

Bibliography of Books

Maurianne Adams et al., eds. *Readings for Diversity and Social Justice: An Anthology on Racism, Sexism, Anti-Semitism, Heterosexism, Classism, and Ableism.* New York: Routledge, 2000.

John Boghosian Arden *America's Meltdown: The Lowest Common-Denominator Society.* Westport, CT: Praeger, 2003.

William J. Bennett *The Broken Hearth: Reversing the Moral Collapse of the American Family.* New York: Doubleday, 2001.

Arthur Asa Berger *Ads, Fads, and Consumer Culture: Advertising's Impact on American Character and Society.* Lanham, MD: Rowman and Littlefield, 2004.

Walter Berns *Making Patriots.* Chicago: University of Chicago Press, 2001.

David Brock *Blinded by the Right: The Conscience of an Ex-Conservative.* New York: Crown, 2002.

J. Alison Bryant, ed. *Television and the American Family.* Mahwah, NJ: Lawrence Erlbaum Associates, 2001.

Patrick J. Buchanan *Death of the West.* New York: St. Martin's Press, 2002.

Stephen L. Carter *God's Name in Vain: The Wrongs and Rights of Religion in Politics.* New York: Basic Books, 2000.

Anne Coulter *Treason: Liberal Treachery from the Cold War to the War on Terrorism.* New York: Crown Forum, 2003.

Chas Critcher *Moral Panics and the Media.* Philadelphia: Open University Press, 2003.

Dick DeVos *Rediscovering American Values.* New York: Dutton, 1997.

Al Franken *Lies and the Lying Liars Who Tell Them: A Fair and Balanced Look at the Right.* New York: E.P. Dutton, 2003.

James G. Gimpel, J. Celeste Lay, and Jason E. Schuknecht *Cultivating Democracy: Civic Environments and Political Socialization.* Washington, DC: Brookings Institution Press, 2003.

Henry A. Giroux *The Abandoned Generation: Democracy Beyond the Culture of Fear.* New York: Palgrave Macmillan, 2003.

Al Gore and
Tipper Gore
Joined at the Heart: The Transformation of the American Family. New York: Henry Holt, 2002.

David Horowitz
The Politics of Bad Faith: The Radical Assault on America's Future. New York: Free Press, 1998.

James Davison Hunter
Culture Wars: The Struggle to Control the Family, Art, Education, Law, and Politics in America. New York: Basic Books, 2000.

M. Thomas Inge
and Dennis Hall
The Greenwood Guide to American Popular Culture. Westport, CT: Greenwood, 2002.

Jessica Kornbluth
and Jessica Papin, eds.
Because We Are Americans: What We Discovered on September 11, 2001. New York: Warner Books, 2001.

Michael Lerner
Spirit Matters. Charlottesville, VA: Hampton Roads, 2000.

Michael Moore
Stupid White Men. New York: ReganBooks, 2002.

Paul K. Moser and
Thomas L. Carson, eds.
Moral Relativism: A Reader. New York: Oxford University Press, 2001.

Cecilia Elizabeth
O'Leary
To Die For: The Paradox of American Patriotism. Princeton, NJ: Princeton University Press, 1999.

Bill O'Reilly
Who's Looking Out for You? New York: Broadway Books, 2003.

William Rivers Pitt
Our Flag, Too: The Paradox of Patriotism. New York: Context Books, 2003.

Norman Podhoretz
My Love Affair with America: The Cautionary Tale of a Cheerful Conservative. New York: Free Press, 2000.

James W. Potter
The 11 Myths of Media Violence. Thousand Oaks, CA: Sage, 2003.

Alissa Quart
Branded: The Buying and Selling of Teenagers. Cambridge, MA: Perseus, 2003.

Daniel W. Rossider
Communication, Media, and American Society: A Critical Introduction. Lanham, MD: Rowman and Littlefield, 2003.

Wendy Shalit
A Return to Modesty: Rediscovering the Lost Virtue. New York: Free Press, 1999.

Robert Singh, ed.
American Politics and Society Today. Malden, MA: Blackwell, 2002.

James B. South, ed.
Buffy the Vampire Slayer and Philosophy: Fear and Trembling in Sunnydale. Chicago: Open Court, 2003.

Karen Struening	*New Family Values: Liberty, Equality, Diversity.* Lanham, MD: Rowman and Littlefield, 2002.
Strobe Talbott and Nayan Chanda	*The Age of Terror: America and the World After September 11.* New York: Basic Books, 2001.
James P. Twitchell	*Lead Us into Temptation: The Triumph of American Materialism.* New York: Columbia University Press, 1999.
Alan Wolfe	*Moral Freedom: The Impossible Idea That Defines the Way We Live Now.* New York: W.W. Norton, 2001.
Howard Zinn	*A People's History of the United States: 1492–Present.* New York: HarperCollins, 2003.

Index